PISCES

The Ultimate Guide to an Amazing Zodiac Sign in Astrology

Contents

Introduction

Like all the signs of the Zodiac, the symbol for Pisces explains a great deal about those who are born under it. Two fish appear to swim in opposite directions, indicating tension in the character of Pisces people.

I prefer to look at the fish differently. I see them as swimming in an eternal loop, ever-rotating around the mysteries of the universe, penetrating and illuminating them. This idea is probably more in line with the dreamy, mystical nature of Pisces.

Ever-seeking the beautiful and the numinous, Pisces people don't spend their time daydreaming for nothing. They're people of creativity and ideas whose imaginations take them places others have no idea are even out there. Like cats, they see what we don't see.

Empathetic to a fault, Pisces wants everyone around them to feel good. They want people in their immediate circle and those on their peripheries to feel as though they belong. Of all the traits of this fascinating sign, empathy is probably one of the most prominent.

But isn't it true that most people with interest in astrology know that? Yes! This is why this book is intended to be a much more intimate exploration of Pisces, and how the people of this sign navigate the treacherous waters of human relationships.

In this book, we'll learn:

> • The astrological reasons for the behavior of Pisces people
>
> • How Pisces people grow into life by interpreting it in their own special way
>
> • How their relationships with people under other signs in the Zodiac play out
>
> • The meaning of rising signs, decanates, and cusps
>
> • Why astrology continues to be turned to by millions to understand other people better and why it's dismissed by just as many

More than a superficial survey of Pisces, this book will help you understand this amazing sign in the zodiac more fully. And if you're a Pisces yourself, you'll be gaining more knowledge about what makes you tick, your relationships, and how you live your life.

I hope you enjoy this in-depth exploration of watery Pisces. Thank you for reading and thank you for your interest in astrology!

Chapter One: Meet Pisces – February 19 – March 20

In our first chapter, we'll meet the Pisces, discovering the astrological nuts and bolts that make them tick. Then, we'll encounter Pisces in their native habitats at work, in their social lives, and at home.

We will begin by examining the semiotics of the sign, consisting of assigned symbols, the ruling planet, and other important details governing Pisces.

Getting a Handle on Pisces

The first thing I want to share with you about Pisces concerns the two fish in the sign's symbol.

These are derived from the Greek myth of Aphrodite/Venus, born from the sea. In Greek mythology, the fish are called "Ichthyocentaurs." These mythical beasts bore the upper body of a human, the forelegs of a horse, with the rest of the body consisting of a fish's tail. A Byzantine writer, Ioannes Tzetzes, is said to have been the first to use the term in the 12th Century. Elsewhere, you'll find the mythical creature described as a "sea-centaur."

These beings can also be found in Syrian mythology and are involved with the birth from the sea of the goddess Astarte.

The symbol of the fish was adopted by the Early Christians to represent Christ. Called the "Ichthys" in Greek, the ancient meaning of the fish is connected to the mythology about water, which emanated from many early belief systems and which became the basis for the Christian Rite of Baptism. The christened is submerged under the water—representing the waters from which the earth was born, in the Book of Genesis—emerging as a new creature, born into the death and the resurrection of Jesus.

In its position as the final sign of the zodiac, Pisces represents the cumulative experiences of all the other 11 signs. This is both a tremendous burden and an extravagant gift. Tied up with ancient beliefs about the world and its creation, Pisces is a sign which represents both death and new life. Its position in the zodiac can be understood to represent the cyclical and ever-changing nature of human life and its mystery.

Pisces represent the completion of the year, and the point at which another orbit around the sun commences.

Feminine? Mileage May Vary

Zodiac signs are considered either feminine or masculine, and Pisces is considered feminine. The sex associated with the signs of the zodiac tends to indicate extroversion versus introversion. We'll be talking about the sexed zodiac in Chapter Seven, especially with respect to the understanding of gendered notions attached to biological sex in the Ancient World.

So, Pisces is an introvert, compounded by the fact this mutable (changeable) sign has water as its elemental signifier, and if there's one thing you can say about water, *it's a changeable element.* While water is indispensable, bringing life to all things, it can also be extremely destructive. But don't let that scare you too much! Just know that the implied duality of the fish can manifest when other planetary circumstances are in play. With Pisces, water is more of a friendly element than anything and not just to Pisces but to those around them.

Pisces shares its status as a feminine sign with Capricorn, Taurus, Virgo, and Scorpio, while the signs Aries, Gemini, Leo, Aquarius, and Leo are considered male. While feminine signs like Pisces are said to be inner-focused, the masculine signs are said to deploy their energies toward the world around them. While the feminine draws in, the masculine strikes out. But this is not an assessment of the intrinsic value or the rich nature of those under these signs. So, signs are sexed to describe their energetic quality. We all carry traits considered either masculine or feminine, living in harmony. But we tend to be raised according to gendered expectations of what it means to be a man or a woman, which can muddy the waters. Again, we'll be having a critical look at the sexed zodiac later on in this book.

Astrology is about humanity, not about the sexes, except in this particular instance, which comes down to us from the Ancient World. That's important to note here, as our anthropological dimorphism (dual expression of humanity via the sexes) is rooted in a gendered understanding of what the sexes mean and how they move through the world. Gender concerns self-expression, which is not governed by biology.

Preview of Chapter Seven: I hereby challenge astrology to abandon sex stereotypes about the nature of biological reality! Let's bring astrology into the 21st Century together!

Neptune and Jupiter

The two planets which rule Pisces are both named for male gods in the Ancient World. Jupiter was considered the Piscean ruling planet by the ancients, but Neptune has since taken its place.

So, how does this work when we're talking about a "feminine" sign? Shouldn't Pisces be ruled by planets named for goddesses?

The explanation perhaps lies in the establishment of male rule in religious life. Before the rise of the major monotheistic religions, women were charged with human spirituality, but all that changed, with the birth of monotheism in Judaism, then Christianity, and finally, Islam.

For Pisces, Neptune makes sense, as this is the planet named for the God of the Seas. You'll see Neptune everywhere you go in Europe but nowhere more frequently than in Rome, Italy, where myriad public art pieces, like the Fontana de Trevi and the magnificent fountains in Piazza Navona, were fashioned in his likeness.

But Neptune was officially discovered in 1846, long after Jupiter was in 1610. Neptune is associated with many aspects of the Piscean personality. Governing intellectual and spiritual life, Jupiter proposes exploration driven by curiosity and fearlessness. Reigning over matters religious and philosophical, it seems a good fit for the nature for Pisces. Their introverted, introspective nature echoes the traits of the planet which rules over their sign.

In the 12th House

As we've discussed earlier, Pisces is the last of all the signs in the zodiac. And each sign, of which there are 12, denotes a unique ambiance. Each house bears in it the sign it represents, and each house in the Pisces sign governs a certain sector of your life. To determine your houses, you must create a chart based on both the date of your birth and the time. We'll explore astrological houses and what they govern in greater detail later in this book, but here are the basics.

• First house—how people read you

This house is concerned with what people see when they look at you. This is the house of first impressions.

How you respond when threatened or venturing into places you've never been is also governed by this house, which is the House of Aries. And Aries is very concerned with the superficial and the self.

• Second house - what matters to you

This is the house of what is important to you in life, with a focus on money and valuables. It also determines who you think about and how you live with money and possessions, and what kind of importance you place on them.

This house represents Taurus, which is concerned with ownership. It also governs how you see yourself and how much you value yourself in relation to other people.

• Third house—how you communicate

This is the "thinking house," determining your communication style and the thought processes which define it. This house governs how you interact with and talk to the people around you, including family members.

Gemini is represented by this house, determining both the nature of your voice and how it's communicated and in the media.

• Fourth house—your foundation

The fourth house represents Cancer, which is all about feelings. The fourth house governs your sense of "home" and what it means, with the moon in charge. How secure you feel in the world and how grounded you are in your sense of self is determined by this sensitive house.

• Fifth house—the child within

The way we are as children is usually carried with us through life, for better or worse. Governing all the best stuff in life from play to pleasure to joy and creativity and romance, here's where your self-expression lives.

Leo is represented by this House. Leo is an active sign that demands you come to the party it's hosting and that you bring that child you once were along for the ride.

- Sixth house—daily life

Representing Virgo, the analytical sign, the sixth house determines how you conduct your daily life, your health, and how you organize yourself. Your problem-solving abilities, habits, and diligence live in this house.

Under this house, you'll also find your beloved pets, your ability to schedule, and your personal routines.

- Seventh house—relationships with others

"Relationships" here can mean everything from partnerships in business to marriages, friendships, and how you manage them.

But enemies are also governed by this house, with vanity and envy under its auspices. This is the house of Libra, so any legal issues that arise in life are influenced by the sign of the scales. "Balance" is the operative word.

- Eighth house—dynamic change and desire

Scorpio is the sign represented by this House, and that sign governs sexuality. But it's not all fun and games here. Crisis is governed by the eighth House, as well as addiction.

This house influences the nature of change and how you respond to it in life. While change means rebirth or transformation, it may also mean death or crisis.

- Ninth house—learning

The ninth house emanates from Sagittarius, which is the zodiac sign of possibilities. Ruling over your spirituality, systems of belief, and personally held philosophy.

Adventurous Sagittarius also governs commerce, culture, publishing languages, and long-distance travel. Optimism and seeing beyond what's in front of your face are traits governed by the ninth House.

• Tenth house—reputation and what you leave behind you

Practical Capricorn is represented in this house, defining what you achieve, your chosen career, and the legacy you leave in the world. The tenth House governs financial success, notoriety, and ambition.

Your relationship to authority is also ruled by this House, as well as your attitude toward the potential in your life for the achievement of various kinds.

• Eleventh house—your hopes, dreams, and purpose

What you most hope for, wish for, and what you see as your life's purpose are all governed by this house, Aquarius.

Your friends, acquaintances and personal networks are determined by the influence of this House. This is the House of connection and community.

• Twelfth house—your spirituality

This, of course, is the house of Pisces. It rules over the sectors of your personality unseen by others, including your secrets and your subconscious.

This is the house in which the self is deconstructed, resulting in spiritual growth. In the deconstructing of the self is the truth of spirit— something ardently sought after by Pisces.

Importantly, your Houses can only accurately be defined by preparing an astrological chart. For this, you must either create a chart for yourself or turn to a professional. If you plan to do this, I strongly suggest that you consult an astrological professional to obtain the most accurate reading possible. No, you can't do an accurate astrological chart without your time of birth, so get that information first! There are many places online to have a chart done, but the most reliable of these is Astro.com.

Gemstones and Colors

Aquamarine is the gemstone most popularly associated with Pisces. But it's not the only one.

Aquamarine is joined by bloodstone, amethyst, jade, jasper, and ruby. Aquamarine is Pisces' planetary stone, specifically referencing the planet Neptune. Its light blue color is reminiscent of the sea. This stone represents Pisces' powerful empathic powers and emotional richness.

Amethyst is a purple gemstone, imparting peace, love, and happiness to the wearer.

Ruby is the talismanic stone associated with Pisces, its bright red color recalling blood and passion. Ruby brings those who wear their wisdom and the ability to live in peace with others.

Internationally acknowledged as a lucky stone, Jade rewards the goodness of the wearer. It's believed that those who are kind and loving will benefit most abundantly from this stone. It represents the heart chakra and brings those who wear it vivid dreams, healing, and a more robust spirituality.

Bringing increased creativity, Bloodstone can help Pisces regain personal power following a life crisis. This stone also enhances Pisces' already highly developed intuitive skills.

Jasper soothes the restless, sensitive, Piscean soul. Assisting Pisces with emotional management, this stone is also rumored to reveal information about past lives to the wearer.

Pisces colors are blue, teal, and variations of purple, lilac, and mauve. Ethereal and watery, picture Pisces drifting into the party in a flowing magenta caftan or a diaphanous, tie-dyed extravaganza from head to toe. Men may not show up in such an extravagantly dramatic outfit, but you can bet they'll be wearing the same palette and probably a few embroidered elements. With Pisces, it's all about wearing your heart on your sleeve in your favorite color!

Now, let's find out about cusps, as these are important, and this section will explain why.

Teetering on the Brink

Being born on the cusp means that you've been born on the boundary between two zodiac signs. If you're a Pisces born on the Pisces-Arie cusp, your birth date falls between March 17 and March 23. And if you're born on the Aquarius-Pisces cusp, it falls between February 15 and February 21.

Cusp people are likely to sense internal conflict due to the fact they're essentially teetering on the brink between two very different signs. Both the examples above have specific names to describe them. The Pisces-Aries cusp can be called the "Cusp of Rebirth", while the Aquarius-Pisces cusp is described as the "Cusp of Sensitivity". Let's examine what being born during these two cusp periods means for "edgy" Pisceans.

The Pisces-Aries "Cusp of Rebirth" presents the intuitive Pisces with the aggressive nature of the first sign of the zodiac. With Pisces being the concluding sign and Aries being the beginning of the 12-sign sequence, this is an Alpha/Omega situation. This is the point at which the astrological wheel turns, and the astrological year begins.

While Pisces longs for peace and communion with all that is, Aries wants to butt heads. Aries is a fire sign, with a continual urge to move ever forward, without hesitation or impediment, and that is not the Pisces way at all!

It is important to note while these two signs are energetic opposites, the Pisces on the cusp benefits with an almost uncanny sixth sense. There's something about the Cusp of Rebirth, which makes the intuitive abilities of a Pisces even more awe-inspiring.

Sensitive Pisces further benefits from being on the cusp by having an enhanced ability to defend themselves when needed. Instead of dissolving into tears of frustration, the Cusp of Rebirth Pisces is much more likely to put up the proverbial dukes and rumble!

The Cusp of Sensitivity—Aquarius-Pisces—Brilliant and innovative, Aquarians bring Pisces born on the Cusp of Sensitivity even more unique energy, combined with exceptional creativity and intuition, which rivals even the abilities of those born on the Cusp of Rebirth.

Free spirits, ever seeking innovation, and new horizons, the Aquarian influence on Pisces on the cusp is profound. The sensitivity of Pisces is tempered by Aquarius. Pisceans born on the Cusp of Sensitivity are also much more able to erect strong boundaries that people take seriously because they're less likely to allow them to be breached.

The influence of Aquarius also focuses dreamy Pisces less on the value of psychic forecasting and more on their powerful intuition. That intuitive aptitude becomes a weapon in the hands of a Pisces born on the cusp with Aquarius.

Later we will move into the more complex aspects of astrology, including rising signs, decanates, and the importance of the planets—especially the moon in astrological charts—to the character of individual Pisceans.

Now that we've covered the astrological nuts and bolts that affect the way this sign moves through the world, let's explore a few of Pisces' most iconic traits, both positive and negative. Not even Pisces are all sunshine and lollipops.

Chapter Two: Who are these People?

"It's tougher to be vulnerable than to actually be tough."

Rihanna (Pisces)

Anyone lucky enough to have a Pisces friend has plenty of stories, and I'm no exception. Knowing a Pisces, whether male or female, is an experience like none other. While not the easiest people to get to know well, they're well worth the effort.

In this chapter, describing classical traits of Pisces, I will paint a picture of a close friend. I hope to explain how a Pisces is most likely to approach life.

After reading the first chapter, you'll understand that mileage may vary from Pisces to Pisces. The role of the other planets in any given Pisces' chart, and where they're born in the sign, is highly influential. Other environmental factors must also be actively and carefully considered.

It's quite reasonable to say that while there are differences between male and female Pisces, sex doesn't have a tendency to change the characteristics of people born under this sign. These differences are less important than the sign itself. Remember that Pisces concludes the zodiac, containing trace attributes and lessons from the preceding 11 signs. This means that Pisces soul is the eldest of all 12. Having traversed through all the other signs to arrive at the karmic terminus of the astrological wheel, the Piscean soul has reached spiritual mastery and wisdom.

It's not all sunshine and roses under the sign of the fish, though. Pisces waters can be just as dark and dysfunctional as those of any other sign.

Tough to be Vulnerable

The quote above from Piscean chanteuse, Rihanna, is so typical of Pisces. While they wear their vulnerability on their sleeves, they do so from a place of strength. This is the gift of wisdom, which all Pisces are heir to.

Vulnerability is represented by the exposure of our emotions. This is a tremendous part of what it means to be a Pisces. This is a sign with little interest in cloaking its feelings. While many read Pisces as slippery—like fish slipping through the water—Pisceans tend to splash as far away as possible, if a confrontation looms. They know all too well that bald confrontation is an emotional exposure that can leave them reeling for days, if not weeks. So, even that "slippery" quality is a manifestation of wisdom. It's both a survival strategy and a boundary.

That's because the Pisces understands the potential pain confrontation can present. Pisces also understands that, when pushed too far, they are perfectly capable of giving it to someone, yanking their chain with both barrels.

Because of this sign's abundant creativity, vulnerability translates almost like a superpower, allowing Pisces to tap into a wellspring of emotional scenarios from which they've learned to share their insights with others via their chosen form of expression.

The empathic nature of Pisces makes them something of a psychic sponge for the currents of emotion around them. In the presence of people with dark energy, Pisces is likely to flee. The discomfort of finding themselves around this type of energy can be extreme.

Their vulnerability makes it impossible for them to spend much time around the toxic, narcissists, attention seekers, liars, and manipulators. With the most porous of emotional boundaries, Pisces can be overwhelmed when in the wrong place at the wrong time, for this very reason. They may just get up and leave without warning if they find themselves face-to-face with someone who sets off their alarm bells.

But the flip side of Pisces' vulnerability is their ability to comfort and nurture those around them. There is no broader shoulder to cry on than that of a Pisces and no ear more willing to listen to your woes.

Remember: Pisces has been there—wherever "there" is.

Understanding without Knowing

Sharing honors with the two other water signs, Cancer and Scorpio, Pisces is undoubtedly the most empathic of all the signs. Pisceans have a unique ability to talk people "off the ledge," understanding what's going on, emotionally, with other people, without being apprised of the situation. They just know.

The friend I mentioned earlier is a perfect example. Her ability to comfort those in crisis is legendary in our circle of friends. She always seems to know what to say and how to approach someone having a rough time. Without being too overbearing, she empathizes with their suffering.

And how else could it be for the Piscean soul, the culmination, and satisfaction of the astrological journey? They have inhabited all the other signs. They have felt all the feelings there is to feel. Perhaps that's why they're so emotionally open—they've learned all the lessons our emotions have to teach us about life; they have already lived what the sufferer is living.

It's said that all human life originated in the ocean. But Pisces is the ocean's messenger. While the rest of us have crawled to shore, Pisces still slaps its tail in the water, admiring the reflection of empathic wholeness. All that exists is part of this sign, and so Pisces' ability to feel what others are feeling is part of the magic of the fish and one reason people misunderstand Pisces so often.

There's something a little uncanny about a being someone able to see within the hearts of others without seeing, understanding them without knowing. There is no analysis. There is only that mysterious ability to know without understanding, through the many incarnations that have come before, as the Pisces soul moves through the zodiac to its terminus.

Pisces knows this life is not forever and that, when it ends, the sea will become the home of all.

Unbound Creativity

While dreaming has a bad name in our highly industrialized and mechanized society, without dreamers, where would we be as a species? It's the dreamers among us who make the changes that bring us forward. Dreamers like Steve Jobs - a Pisces, of course!

And here's where Piscean dreaming has a tremendous impact. With an imagination that never shuts off, Pisces are always searching for the connection between that imagination and the interconnectedness of the Piscean soul.

With the sense that they're connected to all that is and ever has been, Pisces has a plumb line that drills down through human history to discover the roots of truth, beauty, and purpose. Fearlessly, the Pisces are often unaware of where the ideas that pop into their heads come from. Their imaginative intellectual doodling may be called flights of fancy by a few, but Apple stands in testament to the power of Steve Jobs' dreams.

The traditional modes of thinking are, for Pisces, a prison. In the very fabric of their lives, they're able to create new ways of living, seeing, acting, creating, and being in the world that may seem out of step.

They're out of step with social conventions, for one. Again, my friend is a perfect example. She has never been one to stay in a place for too long, preferring to move freely about the world. But she's no tourist. When she finds a place she loves, she stays. She puts down roots for as long as she believes she should rightfully and properly be there, learns the language and the culture, and then she moves on.

One of my favorite quotes from her is this: "People aren't trees." While we may put down roots—as my friend is known to, occasionally —we are not rooted to the spot forever. In her opinion, people are made to move from place to place, experiencing the world from other perspectives and learning from the experience. She finds bliss in this rootlessness, a bliss that provokes the mystery of creativity. She knows she's connected to all that is, and so she lives that truth to the fullest.

This willingness to step outside the bounds of what's considered "normal" inspires my friend, allowing her to translate her dreaming, intuition, and sense of connectedness into her work—which is, of course, creative.

These are three of the dominant, classical, positive traits of the Pisces. But as any Pisces will happily tell you, the universe is held in tension. Where there is light, there is also darkness.

So, get ready for Pisces' negative traits!

When Fish Get Cold

Piscean sensitivity is a double-edged sword. While their sensitive nature allows them to "read" people and to navigate social situations based on their ability to do so, it also makes them highly susceptible to being hurt or offended.

The Pisces connects with people they've "read" as safe to be around. This can lead to the idealization of the people they have connected with in any capacity. And when that idealization happens, Pisces will respond poorly to perceived slights.

A slight can be anything from canceling a date or social outing at the last minute to not calling when you said you would. Because you're on the Piscean pedestal as a friend, lover, family member, or colleague, they will shut down, forcing the person who's disappointed them to make the first move.

But if you've messed with Pisces deliberately, you will encounter a wall of utter silence. Once the Pisces has identified you as a liar, manipulator, cheater, or any other type of person the Pisces actively avoids, don't even expect an acknowledgment of your existence.

You have died to them. You are no more. You are an ex-person.

When the fish goes cold, it stays cold. If you're not the person Pisces thought you were, you will encounter the dark chill of the ocean's depths, and you'd better get used to it because there's no going back. Pisces does not tolerate people who live by any code of conduct other than one founded on decency and kindness.

But if whatever happened between you was not intentional on your part, Pisces will thaw out eventually. A word to the wise:—when dealing with Pisces, be exactly who you say you are. Pretending to be something or someone you're not will earn you the eternal contempt of Pisces.

And I know this to be 100% true because I've seen my Pisces friend do this with more than one person. One was a cheating ex-husband. She did not attempt to work the relationship out. She did not give him a second chance. She moved out, started over, and divorced him. Those who mention his name in her presence regret it. There was also the case of the friend who threw her overboard for the sake of a lover. My Pisces friend had taken one look at the guy and knew at once what he was—an opportunist, trying to get a free ride on her friend's back. She tried to explain this, but her friend wouldn't listen, so Pisces walked out the door and never looked back. To this day, she doesn't speak to this friend, who kicked the opportunistic boyfriend out of her luxury condo seven times in nine months, took him back, then kicked him out again. During their split, he spent time with two other women, and behaved in the same manner. My Pisces friend knew all this, and we talked about it. She said "People choose what they believe they deserve and what she believes she deserves a gigolo."

The matter was never spoken of again, and to this day, this friend is not mentioned. When Pisces slams the door and you're on the other side, don't expect to get back through it.

"Where the heck did I put my phone?"

With the Piscean propensity to avoid the cruelty of the world, they can be found dreaming and are often by dreaming comes a flighty, which can be unsettling for others who cross their path.

It's one thing to be disorganized. It's something entirely more problematic when you're leaving your cell phone in the backseat of a taxi, just because you were preoccupied, or you leave your car keys in plain sight, just to forget where you put them five minutes later.

And this is a common Pisces negative trait. In fact, this is one trait that can make people around them crazy. When important items like a cell phone are lost, all hell can break loose rather quickly.

But they don't do it on purpose. Pisces' mind is always full of thoughts, dreams, and visions, so their cell phones are the furthest things from their minds, most of the time. That's especially true when they're gazing out the window at the world going by without a care to be had.

Pisceans struggle with this tendency that can cost them jobs, friends, and lovers. It's frustrating for those around them because Pisces tends to take losing important items like cell phones in stride, usually laughing off the loss.

Enter my Piscean friend again. While, like all Pisces, she's adorable, fun, intelligent, and witty, she's also scatterbrained. She has lost at least three cell phones in the past two years. I bought her a cell phone tether for her purse for Christmas. When she saw it, she was overjoyed, saying, "Well, you know I need this, right?" We laughed heartily at that one.

But she doesn't use it, which is classic Piscean behavior.

And that's why people who know and love Pisces stick around. They're who they are, and most of us find my friend's scatterbrained behavior endearing. It also makes for a great dinner party conversation! And no, Pisces won't mind if you laugh at their antics. They'll laugh right along with you.

Mañana!

One of Pisces' greatest life challenges is a tendency to be lazy. Sorry to be so blunt, but it must be said. Ask any Pisces you know whether they're lazy, and they may protest to endless industry, but only momentarily. In the end, they'll agree that they're only too happy to lay about and dream.

To be fair, though, Piscean laziness isn't just about being distracted by their active imaginations or not wanting to work. What it's really about is boredom. This is the leading reason that Pisces needs to choose the right line of work. A job that doesn't interest them is a living hell for Pisces.

Unfortunately, our culture continues to advance the notion of hard work as the panacea for all that ails us. And while it's true that working hard to achieve something is noble, it's not necessarily the way a Pisces sees life unfolding. Not all hard work is interesting, noble, or rewarding. Hard work is just backed being broken to make other people wealthy, and Pisces doesn't play that.

The moral universe of the Pisces bends toward justice. It's the nature of the fish. It's crucial that Pisces not be tempted by economic circumstance or a hefty paycheck to sign on for work they don't emotionally connect to.

My Pisces friend has learned this about herself. She once told me that she'd taken more than one job out of sheer desperation to get the rent paid, resenting having to do so bitterly. A bitter Pisces is a Pisces who you'll find staring out the window instead of doing what he or she is being paid to do.

And laziness isn't the only thing that can have a damaging effect on Piscean productivity. Procrastination is another challenge for this sign. If they don't want to do something, they'll put off doing it until the last possible moment. Whatever that something is, it will creep down the Piscean "to do" list until it drops right off the page, as Pisces has forgotten about it. This can create a lot of unnecessary conflict in work settings.

For Pisces, the environment at work is extremely important. They need engagement and stimulation to keep them interested in what they're doing. More than that, they need to believe in what they're doing and find joy and satisfaction in whatever that is.

So, there you have it. These are the most notable and universal traits of people born under the sign of Pisces. Other facets of Pisces will pop up as we move through the book, but these are the most iconic.

Nobody's perfect. We all have our flaws and our growing edges. It should give us all comfort that even the spiritually aware and karmically experienced Pisces has a few warts among their silvery scales.

In our next chapter, we'll stalk Pisces in their natural habitats at work, play, and home. Let's see if you recognize anyone!

Chapter Three: Peeking into the Spheres of Pisces

The woman with the silk flower in her hair. The man who's always smiling and remembers no one birthday. The teen who fills notebook after notebook with intricate drawings. The child who seems to know much more about life than she should.

Any of them may be a Pisces.

In this chapter, we'll peek into the world of Pisces. These brief portraits summarize Piscean behaviors in the three dominant spheres of life—work, home, and leisure. We'll look at what to expect from Pisces in each of these contexts. Let's start our journey into the world of Pisces with work.

The Pisces Boss

Many of you will find the title of this section oxymoronic. But then, you'd be forgetting about Pisceans like the USA's first President, George Washington, Director Spike Lee, and Steve Jobs.

So, while many Pisces shrink from the spotlight and the extreme level of responsibility inherent in leadership, that's not true of all Pisces. Again, influences on their sign, like rising signs and the moon they're born under, have a tremendous impact on temperament. The moon can have a striking impact on any of the signs of the zodiac. Many say it's the most important element of the astrological birth chart, and others go so far as to say that the moon sign is more important than the sun sign.

The Pisces boss exists, and sometimes, you'll be surprised to hear that leaders you know and interact with are fish. It seems to out of character, and yet, it's an undeniable reality.

But it may only be a reality when the Pisces has found the niche that highlights all the most prized qualities of this zodiac sign. That's when Pisces' unquenchable passion comes out to play, never tiring of the work, never failing to inspire, and always a dynamic influence on those who work with them.

One of the most compelling attributes of the Pisces boss is the absence of micro-management. A Pisces boss won't be found standing behind you, trying to find errors in your work or screaming at you for coming in a few minutes late. That's not their style.

Their style is to "read" their employees to make sure that they're getting everything they need to recognize their potential. Pisces, who struggle with procrastination or laziness, are keenly aware of what coworkers need to stay fully engaged. Of all the other signs, a Pisces is most likely to recognize boredom and bullying, when it occurs on their watch.

The Pisces is oriented toward the good in matters of human relations and fervently desires to make those they supervise feel not only comfortable in the workplace but valued and appreciated. They know it hurts to be overlooked. They know it hurts to be ignored and misunderstood. It happens to them a lot.

So, the Pisces boss is like a lighthouse seen in stormy seas— reassuring, inspiring, and ready to encourage employees to be their very best. The Pisces boss sees well ahead. That ability to see what others don't, while unnerving, is also the hallmark of leaders who change the world for the better and transform workplaces from productivity mills to centers of excellence.

Pisces understands that when their unique vision of a certain project or goal is articulated to employees, that they catch fire, and so, Pisces' communication skills are deployed actively to ensure that all employees share in that unique vision and its purpose.

Because the Pisces boss is an intuitive, empathic leader, they know employees need to be liberated from arcane regulations to do their best work. Pisces knows that when this happens, their employees will become part of a leadership team that is collaborative instead of hierarchical.

Instead of micro-managing employees, the Pisces boss lets them out of the barn and into the field, knowing that free-range employees produce more satisfying results and those results are more likely to conform with the vision in play when they're not smothered.

But make no mistake; this isn't about being "nice." A consultative leader who encourages a less marked hierarchy is strategically aware. This leader understands that hanging over people doesn't get the job done; intuitive Pisces knows exactly how to extract the desired performance and results.

And all that sounds a little like Steve Jobs, doesn't it? Well, it does–and doesn't. Steve Jobs has also seen a heavy-handed leader, but he is undeniably the most successful entrepreneur of the last half-century. Many variables in astrology can impact the characteristics of the signs, so you may see a different outcome. At the same time, there are overarching truths that usually bear out.

I'm not about to lie—there are downsides to having a Pisces boss, too. I've just mentioned Steve Jobs, who was known to centralize power around his office, demanding total control from the top down. It should be told that Steve Jobs was born with an Aries moon, and Mars was also in Aries. The aggressive ram is known for butting heads, and Jobs rejected the contention that employees had any right to do that with him. He was known simultaneously as "mean and intimidating" and "inspiring and motivating." Keep him in mind as you read the rest of this section.

The Pisces is not keen on being the bearer of bad news—especially the news that an employee has been fired. Administrative nuts and bolts are the biggest bore in the world to the Pisces boss. Functions like performance reviews and payroll cause the Pisces boss's eyes to glaze over in about 10 seconds flat. A Pisces boss may even slip out the side door to avoid such important facets of working life.

Just know that if you work with a Piscean manager or other leader, you'll see the best of humanity and also a little childish flight from responsibility. What the Pisces boss needs more than anything is administrative support to *get the boring end of the job done.* When this is in place, a Pisces boss is inspirational, productive, and exceptional.

HINT: Just don't try to drive the agenda. That Pisces tail may well come out to slap you back into line!

The Pisces Employee

Much like the Pisces boss, the Pisces employee is a force of a creative nature. There is no sign more imaginative, bringing innovative and novel thinking to any table. While the corporate world or politics might seem like the last place, you'd find a Pisces, they're out there. The late Congressman John Lewis, a lifelong civil rights firebrand, was a Pisces, as was the late Senator Ted Kennedy and—believe it or not—Senate majority leader Mitch McConnell.

Pisces individualism and disinterest in conformity for the sake of "fitting in" is what makes them valuable assets in the workplace. These brilliantly unconventional thinkers might not be at home in chartered accounting, but wherever new ways of doing things are welcome, they'll excel. And who knows, a Pisces might invent chartered accounting software that makes the entire affair less boring!

The adaptability of the Pisces is where employers will find a star. Wherever Pisces go is home, so their ability under this star sign to turn on a dime is certainly a selling point. Part of that adaptability is Pisces' tendency to welcome change as a cure for the mundane. Easily bored, Pisces love it when you move the goalposts! While change is unwelcomed by many, Pisces embraces it, making them extremely easy to work with.

Any employer who can harness the limitless potential of the Piscean imagination, creativity, and adaptability will benefit tremendously. But many employers are conventional thinkers stuck in a mechanistic and rules-based past. This can create a lot of problems for Pisces at work.

For this reason, the Pisces should think about careers like consulting or freelancing that offer them the freedom they need to grow and to know satisfaction in their working lives.

Naturally, the creative arts are a Piscean playground, but here are a few other careers which fit the temperament of the fish well.

- **Filmmaker**—The Pisces imagination is tailormade for Tinsel Town.

- **Counselor** - The empathic nature of Pisces makes them ideal for this role. Their ability to "read" people and to feel with others are prerequisites.

- **Caregiver**—Compassionate to a fault, Pisces make exceptional caregivers and nurses.

- **Charity**—Pisces' passion comes out to play in this sector, driving their ability to bring in those donations, deploying their exceptional communication skills

- **Marketing**—Companies who hire a Pisces to craft their branding via marketing and advertising have hired a genius who will build a consistent, powerful brand. Pisces love to bring the unseen to life and creating a persona for a commercial brand is exactly that kind of magic.

There are so many types of work were Pisces can excel. The trick is finding that special place that represents the perfect fit for these unconventional, exceptional people.

Pisces at Play

You're at a party. The music's playing, the drinks are flowing, and everyone's having a terrific time. You look around the patio to see who's out there, and you see a man sitting quietly, sipping a cold drink, smiling, and enjoying the scene before him.

As you watch, he raises his hand and waves at a woman across the room. Seeing him a wave, she stops in mid-conversation, excuses herself, and hurries over to greet the man, as though compelled by the sheer force of his personality.

This is how the Pisces does parties. Not the most social of the signs, Pisces will not be that "life of the party" who starts conversations with random people. Pisces will socialize with those at the party willing to socialize with them—preferably making the first move. That wave across the room? That's about as far as Pisces goes until feeling more comfortable about the overall social whirl around them.

That Pisces friend I introduced to you earlier in this book is a perfect example of the foregoing. I have been to many parties where she's also been a guest. And you know what? At almost every party, she has sat in the same chair all night, rising only to replenish her drink, hit the snack table, and visit the washroom. Despite that, almost every single person in the room went over to where she was sitting and chatted with her. By the end of the party, she was surrounded by others, all of whom were discussing the current state of the world.

While my friend is quite a middling consumer of alcoholic beverages, that may not be said of all Pisces, by any means. Pisces are either a teetotaler (having learned their lesson about booze) or a madcap, dancing on the pool table with a lampshade on their head. This is the default truth about Pisces at a party.

Part of that truth is the pleasure Pisces takes in observing other people. This is Pisces' most beloved party game. Capable of picking up on the emotional landscape of others, Pisces takes mental notes about who they might like to meet and chat with, who to avoid like the plague, and who might be having a bit of a rough time and need a little support.

And Pisces will most likely wind up being the person to provide that support and a shoulder to cry on when the boozy, cathartic tears come later in the evening.

They'll often be found enjoying the music wafting through the room, the sound of laughter, and the pleasure of those surrounding them.

But when Pisces indulges in the social lubricant known as alcohol, he might propose a game of spin the bottle—especially if he's emptied the bottle.

Something Pisces should avoid is becoming dependent on substances. Trying to make social interaction less about competing emotions and more about the people surrounding them and having fun. Because of their finely tuned empathy, Pisces may believe they need liquid courage to cleave the perilous waters of social situations. It helps them dull the energies coming at them, and focus on enjoying their time, instead.

While it has a place, Pisces needs to be careful not to become enmeshed in behaviors like substance abuse. Pisces' potential for addiction to drugs and alcohol can be legendary, with the late Elizabeth Taylor standing as *Exhibit A*. When Pisces know the dangers, they're able to enjoy parties to the fullest—especially when their environment is filled with fun and laughter!

Pisces will run to the dance floor alone, when the mood is right, and the rest of the party will follow. Again, my Pisces friend is always the first to hit the dance floor and has been known to zone out completely, as she closes her eyes and moves blissfully to the music.

Although she could never be described as the life of the party, she is most certainly can be described as the soul.

Pisces at Home

The main goals of Pisces are balance, tranquility, comfort, and beauty.

Spiritually attuned Pisces conceptualizes their living space as a sanctuary from the world, where they can kick back, relax, and let the groove move them. There is nothing more important for Pisces, who needs time to recharge their batteries in a nurturing, pleasant space that speaks to them.

An interesting feature of the Pisces way of being in the world is that their home is something like an extension of them. You might even think of the Pisces home as a cocoon.

A firsthand look into the Pisces mindset about their home living habits comes from my friend. Her home is an oasis of warmth and cushy comfort. Color and art fill every room, and much of the art you'll see on her walls is "outsider" art. This is art made by those who normally get little attention; she loves the originality these works. She likes supporting an unseen, unacknowledged art community. Again, the empathy of the Pisces drives even aesthetic choices.

Going even deeper, it's interesting to consider a bit of what signifies home to the Pisces. My friend, as a child, would travel with her family to various locations in her city. She often noticed small groves of trees here and there and used to fantasize about living in them on her own. To her, this was the ultimate lifestyle. Of course, people grow and change. She'd always had a dream of living by a rushing river, with trees lining it on either side and birds flitting through the trees' dense branches. She now lives by a river, in a small, comfortable home.

In the Pisces home, you'll find pets—usually more than one and often adopted out of an animal support/rescue agency. There is no such thing as a Pisces who can ignore the cries of kittens and puppies. They might not give them all a home, but Pisces will never pass by an animal in need, so a Pisces home will always be graced by the gentle presence of animals, from birds to dogs and cats to baby goats.

Pisces people love being in their homes. Taking great care to decorate to their tastes as, habitually, they spend a great deal of time there. Expect beautiful, rich color. The walls will all be painted and not necessarily with the blues and greens of the ocean. Pisces also adores the colors seen in the natural world beyond the water element, finding inspiration in the colors of flowers, plants, the sunset, sunrise, and the bright yellow of the sun itself.

Expect throw cushions. There's no avoiding them in a Pisces household, and you can bet that Pisces has a memory foam bed topper or mattress. Comfort and self-nurture are so crucial to sensitive Pisces' wellbeing. They love the sense that their home is a world that may only be fully understood by themselves, their beloved pets, and their closest friends.

You may even see your Pisces friends and neighbors decorating their walls with colorful murals and designs. While not everyone may understand this practice, Pisces understands the home as the root of the soul, where they live in perfect contentment and peace. In that nurturing, regenerating state, they ready themselves for what's expected of them in the world.

Married or cohabiting Pisceans will need quiet time to dream or practice their chosen art. While embracing and loving, Pisces can only sustain the level of intensity required by a relationship when able to enjoy ample time alone. So, the Pisces home is one of great love. But it's also one where respect for the individual needs of both partners is paramount. If Pisces' need for time alone is respected, harmony will reign in their peaceable kingdom. If not, Pisces becomes withdrawn, resenting their partner's inability to allow them the regenerative time they so desperately need. The Greta Garbo's of the zodiac, Pisces "want to be alone," as it's what keeps their spirit in balance.

And you'll almost always find Pisces at home. People born under this sign are what I like to call "semi-social." They love their social time, but without their precious time alone, they wither. When given the space, they need in their private oasis of calm and eye-appealing pleasure, they'll return to social life well-rested and ready to engage.

Only the closest of Pisces' friend group will be invited to share in the delights of the Pisces home. Extremely private and selective about their associations, Pisces operates on trust. When trust is not in place, don't expect an invitation to share a bottle of wine on their cozy terrace, crowded with plants, and awash with homey comforts.

Pisces is a sign with many levels, creating the layers of an Old Soul like none other found in the zodiac. Those who work, play, and live with these cosmically attuned creatures wouldn't want to exist in a world without them. Many of us have spirit animals. The lucky among us have Pisceans to guide us.

In our next chapter, we'll look at the Pisces child and how parents can support them growing into the unique people they are.

Chapter Four: Bringing up Baby Pisces

The Pisces child is sometimes a bit of a mystery to parents. All children are a little weird, to be sure, but Pisces out-weirds every other kid on the planet!

My Pisces friend is a perfect example. The only girl in her family, she was always a little different. For one, she rarely cried as an infant. She was not given to the epic tantrums of most toddlers, either. Quiet and watchful, she observed everything she saw and everyone she saw.

Learning to read by the age of two, she was remarkably thirsty to understand the world around her. She wanted to do everything there was to do, studying piano, ballet and painting.

From the time she could talk, it was clear that she was imaginative, as she was always the neighborhood ringleader when it was time for the kids to put on a show. She encouraged her playmates to do what they were best at, which often included singing, dancing or putting on a show.

By the time she got to high school, she was even more of a force of nature, sticking her finger in every pie of knowledge she could find, especially if that pie was concerned with creativity or spirituality. She constantly wrote, inventing characters and little worlds for her hyperactive imagination to inhabit.

She's told me that one of her favorite shows while growing up was I Dream of Jeannie. She loved it because Jeannie lived in an exotic-looking bottle lined with cushions. It never occurred to her that her "master" would send her into the bottle when she was naughty and refuse to let her out. Critical thinking didn't enter into it, though. Neither did the abusive patriarchal overtones of keeping a woman in a bottle. Rather, she focused on the privacy of the space and the coziness of it. That's Pisces for you; it was all about that exotic bottle, with its plentiful, luxurious throw cushions for my friend!

Not Your Average Bear

Pisces children are evidence of Plato's claim that all people are born bearing the knowledge of previous lives. They have a knowing quality not seen in other children. This correlates to the position of the sign at the end of the karmic astrological cycle. All knowledge gained in the other signs is carried within their little souls. How they express that reality is exactly as I described in the case of my friend. Their eyes are always looking. Their minds are always inquiring.

Piscean creativity is a huge part of who children born under this sign are. Pisces children will manifest their creativity early in life, demanding constant encouragement, freedom to explore, and the art supplies they need to let their active imaginations run wild.

While Pisces children make friends easily, they're also content to stay in their own little worlds, finger painting, banging away on a toy piano, or dancing to their favorite tunes on the radio. And if they dance, you'd better watch and then, applaud!

And, like all other Pisces, your fish baby is sensitive. Easily hurt and discouraged from shining as they know they're born to, your support, as a parent, is crucial to the healthy development of the Pisces child. They need you to tell them they can choose creativity and call on it as an emotional and spiritual wellspring all their lives.

Take care of your emotional setting around your Pisces child. Born as mega-empaths, they will often cleave to your emotions to reinforce their connection to you and further, to comfort you. They know when you're not feeling quite right, and they'll be only too happy to join you in your temporary funk. So, it's important that you temper your emotions around them.

Of course, because you're the adult in the relationship, that doesn't go both ways, so your baby Pisces will tell you how they're feeling. Open about their emotions, they want you to know when they're upset or hurt. Pisces aren't shy about letting others know when they're not happy.

In our post-emotional world, that's often an unwelcome trait. But with Pisces, feelings are important, and sharing them with those they trust even more so. While you should support the right of your child to express less than ideal emotions, it's also crucial that you talk to them about emotional management, and what behaviors are expected outside the home.

A Pisces child at school will always be the first to stand up for someone being bullied. They'll be the first to comfort another child in tears, and they won't stand for meanness, lying, or manipulation of any kind. This is one of Pisces' most noble traits—advocacy for others, which springs from the sign's endless compassion.

Sometimes, the Piscean imagination can be a little overwhelming. Many are a little taken aback by the stories Pisces children tell, so filled with detail and adventure; they almost seem like delusions. But don't worry, this is normal for Pisces children. Great outlets for their storytelling are creative writing or creating and improvising impromptu plays with their family and friends. Pisces children will entertain you at the drop of a hat.

My friend tells a story of once escaping from her mother's grasp following her bath and racing to the living room, still wet and completely naked. She then launched herself into a wild dance performance as her father yelled that she was blocking the football game on television, and her brothers rolled on the floor laughing.

One thing's for sure. When you parent a Pisces child, the only dull moments are those your child spends in the private world they love to retreat to. These, you will come to be grateful for. Pisces children are also big talkers, always ready to tell you about what they've learned, their new friend, or their latest fantasy project. They will rotate childhood love interests on the regular, breaking up, making up, flitting from favorite to favorite like the little butterflies they are.

What the Pisces child sees is learned. As visual learners, they pick up things quickly. This will typify their learning style throughout their lives, so encourage them by boning up on visual learning. Learn more about it in the Resources section at the end of this book.

Something genuinely wonderful about the Pisces child is their natural tendency to want to help. While other children hang back, the Pisces will immediately offer to lend a hand.

"Me" and "mine" aren't part of Pisces Baby's vocabulary. They love to share what they have with others. When they see that someone around them doesn't have something everyone else has, they'll do what they can to fix the problem. They are socialists by nature, who believe that everything should be shared with everyone else and that no one should go without while others have more than they need.

As I said earlier, the Piscean moral universe bends toward justice naturally, and that starts as soon as they're able to reason and to note inequality and injustice in their immediate environment.

One of the most endearing traits of the Piscean child is their love of cuddling. This tells them, clearly and unequivocally, that they're loved. Your cuddles are prized by your Pisces child. A lack of them can stunt their development, so be extravagant in showing your water baby how much you love them.

Get your little Pisces outdoors often. Pisces love the natural world, with all its colors, textures, and scents. They love to experience nature, explore bugs, and learn about everything concerned with animals, plants, and flowers. Their curiosity is endless.

If there were a childhood mantra for Pisceans, it would be "don't fence me in." Pisces love its freedom to dream, explore, create, and go to the places their imaginations take them. You may not always understand your fishy little person, but a Pisces child will richly bless with surprise after surprise, bringing the fruits of imagination and fancy into your life.

Give them all the unstructured time they need to pursue their secret worlds, curiosity, and creativity. You'll find that they're most comfortable with either a small group of other children or on their own. As I've related, Pisceans are "semi-social." They can't be forced into a mold that doesn't fit them. Trying to do that is the wrong approach.

Pisces children are also, unfortunately, subject to bullying at times by other children. My Piscean friend experienced this as a child and throughout high school. Even in adulthood, she's sometimes bullied by grown women at work. Sensitive Pisces is a favorite target of bullies. But children in this sign will stand up for themselves as much as they will for other children when the moment presents itself. Sometimes, they shock even themselves with the ferocity of their counterattack. This can lead to unfortunate incidents on the playground. That may take a little finesse on the part of parents. Your job is to instill in your child that there are better ways of dealing with a bully than hitting him over the head with a twirling baton.

True story. My Piscean friend answered a bully this way in third grade. A bully threw a chair at her when the teacher had left the classroom, and she responded by cracking him over the head with her newly gifted baton. She was sent home from school for her efforts. The bully was not. Because when the Pisces child goes off, neutron bombs pale in comparison!

While expressing anger so viscerally can be a problem, it's important to understand that Pisceans internalize negative emotions. This isn't a healthy response to negative emotions. Retaining those feelings is corrosive. Because of this, be sure to work with your Pisces child on containing their temper and also on learning to name and release negative emotions.

You can also spend time with them when they come to you complaining of controlling schoolmates, or manipulative, mendacious ones. Even in childhood, Pisces children have no time for people who engage in such behaviors. Remind them that many people are best bullying.

All this will serve your water baby well in life.

In our next chapter, we will be diving into the adventurous love life of Pisces, exploring their compatibility with other signs. Their style of loving, which is Byzantine in its complexity, boundless in its practice, and thrilling to those lucky enough to know love with this sensual sign.

Chapter Five: Pisces in Love

There is no romantic more hopeless than Pisces. Pisces lives and breathes romance, dreaming of sharing themselves and their lives with a cherished other.

The intensity of the Pisces in love is something not everyone is prepared for. It can seem almost surreal how far they're willing to go to give their all to those they love. Experiencing love with a Pisces is a once in a lifetime experience that has no equal.

Intuitive and spiritual, Pisces reads their lover like a book and then translates what they've read into that person's needs. So be sure you're serious. Because when the Pisces reads any hint of deception or falsehood, they will be shattered, and they will make sure that you share in at least a small portion of the pain you've caused.

Pisces are not people to trifle with. The scars of love can run deep in them, creating rafts of scar tissue that can be opened easily when they detect that you're being dishonest or equivocating with them.

But if you're the real thing, you'll be enveloped in an unparalleled experience of love, replete with the soaring emotions of two beating hearts that won't be stilled. The honest lover with serious intentions is the key to Piscean bliss.

For those reading who have become enchanted by a sensual Pisces, remember that you're the one who must make the approach. Shy Pisces would never presume to do so. That's a small price to pay to experience the fullness of what romantic love is all about. Because you've hooked this fish, you're in for the most delightful experience of your life. And Pisces will remain at your side, even when things go wrong. The emotional investment they make in their partners is not made lightly. It's made for the long haul. For Pisces, the heart and its ways are second nature, and love is all there is.

Let's visit the other signs of the zodiac to discover which of them is most compatible with the most romantic and emotionally available of all the signs.

Aries (March 21-April 19)

Probably the most aggressive of all the signs of the zodiac, Aries can be described as ambitious and bold.

Drawn to each other like magnets, there's chemical attraction aplenty between gentle Pisces and the audacious ram. Aries will move heaven and earth to get at Pisces. But that's Aries. These guys get what they want.

The problem for a dreamy Pisces is that the energy of the ram can be as destructive as it is energetic. Tending to insensitivity, Pisces will have difficulty maintaining emotional balance in a relationship with someone born under Aries.

Sexually, Aries loves sex as an athletic event. There's little of the tender romance that Pisceans live for. With compromise, this part of an Aries can encouraged, but does the ram sound interested in compromise?

As with everything else in astrology, the star sign can be tempered by other elements present in the birth chart, like the moon your love interest is born under.

However, Aries may make for a fun Pisces fling, but there's little to suggest that the opposing energies of these two signs can coexist in loving harmony in the context of a relationship.

Taurus (April 20 — May 20)

Represented symbolically by the bull, this star sign loves serenity and sensuality. While reliable and of an inherently stable disposition, Taurus also believes in the principle of mañana—don't rush these bovine behemoths. They prefer to take their time, relax, and take in the sounds, scents, and scenery.

Pisces and Taurus can be serenely happy together, so long as Taurus doesn't attempt to change Pisces. Flexibility is not Taurus's strongest suit. But if Taurus accepts Pisces dreamy, freewheeling ways, there's a lot of potential in this match.

The stability of the bull is a wonderful complement to Pisces. Knowing what they want and when they want it helps Pisces focus on the here and now, instead of the ethers beyond the earth.

One recommendation for this pairing is the dedication both signs have to loyalty and commitment. In addition, both the fish and ram are reserved and introverted, with both tending to a sentimentality that brings mutual joy.

Pisces is deeply connected to the emotional component of sex, while Taurus focuses on its physical nature. While this may sound like a roadblock, it represents the ying-yang of coupling that can bring great happiness to both partners. Both understand sex as a serious matter, representing the expression of a love bond between two people.

In summary, Pisces in love with Taurus often finds the blissful realization of their dream, and if both partners are aware of and willing to work on their differences, this match has the potential to last a lifetime.

Gemini (May 21-June 20)

Like the two fish, the twins of Gemini represent duality. But they also represent a dynamic and active sign that can't find enough hours in the day to do everything they have in their fevered imaginations to do.

The problem here is that the vitality of Gemini brings with it a tendency to flip from one priority to another at the drop of a dime. Pisces can be thrown off balance by this, and that disorientation can be the source of pain for the sensitive fish.

The activity level of Gemini is also something of a problem for Pisces. The fish needs time to recharge their batteries, and the hyperactive nature of the twins will leave them feeling depleted.

While Gemini is sexually passionate, they often regard their sexuality as a toy. And they may include sensitive Pisces in that column, much to Pisces' detriment. Sex is much more than fun for Pisces, having strong emotional and spiritual components. While Gemini will appear fly-by-night to Pisces, Pisces will seem a bit of a millstone to Gemini.

The energies of these two signs may be mitigated by other factors in the birth chart, but ultimately, they work against one another, making for an unfavorable outcome.

Cancer (June 21-July 22)

If Pisces has something like a twin in the rest of the zodiac, it's Cancer. Represented by the crab, Cancer boasts a similar ability to read the emotional currents in the surrounding people. At home in both earthly pursuits and those of the spirit, Cancer is a truly excellent match for Pisces.

Sexually, this is a match made in heaven and mandated by the stars. Dreamy, tender, romantic, and full of welcome surprises, the fish and crab know exactly how to make each other happy.

The spiritual, emotional, creative, and intellectual bond between Pisces and Cancer is the epitome of holistic, healthy sexuality that satisfies both partners on every level of their beings.

Cancer provides an anchor in the real world for Pisces. While Pisces doesn't care to plan, Cancer is concerned with creating the right conditions for the match to thrive into the future.

This is an exceptional pairing, providing both partners with the bliss, emotional satisfaction, and intuitive—almost psychic—connection both crave.

For money, this is one of Pisces' best shots at the sort of love they desire; love that's almost supernatural.

Leo (July 23-August 22)

Many call people born under this sign the narcissists of the zodiac, and that's not far wrong. Expect Leo not only to claim the spotlight but demand it. Dramatic and expressive, you can't miss the lion. Reigning over all the other signs, Leo doesn't play second fiddle to anyone.

Because Leo likes to lead and control every aspect of their lives, they'll probably want that in your relationship, too. This, for obvious reasons, can be a problem in a Leo-Pisces match.

Sensitive Pisces won't care for Leo's steam roller approach to life, under which are squashed Piscean autonomy, along with Pisces' vibrant emotions. Pisces also is an introvert, while Leo is the extroverted life of every party they go to, in the spotlight from start to finish. This tendency can crush sensitive Pisces.

The success of a match between Pisces and Leo rests on Leo's willingness to temper their need for attention. Pisces may also have difficulty with the materialistic nature of Leo.

Sexually, these two find much to enjoy in each other. Leo's intensity and theatricality complement Pisces' love of fantasy, bringing both sexual satisfaction. Beyond that, this is a match that will require a great deal of accommodation and compromise from both parties.

Virgo (August 21-September 22)

Perfectionist Virgo is rooted in the material world. Practical, logical, and consistent, the Virgo loves to spend time making themselves masters of whatever they strive to master.

Cogito ergo sum—I think, therefore I am—is Virgo's mantra. On the other hand, Pisces *feel.* This is one of the greatest challenges of a match between these two. While Virgo relies on the intellect to guide, Pisces' intuition is their compass for navigating the world.

With feet firmly planted on the ground, Virgo's analytical nature mystifies Pisces, whose primary concerns are the meaning of things and the potential inherent in each day. This drives the practical, calculating Virgo mentally.

Pisces can be maddening for the painstaking Virgo, but Pisces may also be capable of balancing the obsessive-compulsive nature of the sign, while Virgo may be able to reign in a few of Pisces "less desirable" traits, organizing and tempering them.

Physically, sex for this pairing is excellent. Both partners will be highly satisfied by the emotional bonding their combined sexuality can create. But Virgo's analytical nature can get in the way, as they'll always be wondering if this is the best they can do.

And frankly, that's not enough for emotional Pisces, whose commitment to their partners is all-encompassing.

Libra (September 23-October 22)

Fun fact: only Libra is denoted by a manmade symbol. The scales represent the balanced nature of this sign, and people born under it reflect the nature of the scales, which is symmetry in all things.

While this pairing is desirable, both signs require a partner who is somewhat more stable and stronger. With both being intensely idealistic, this celestial coupling might be better off with a little more real. As always, this factor may be mitigated by other influences in the charts of both.

Libra's diplomacy, combined with the Pisces preference for flexibility, can be at odds. But fortunately, the communicative styles of both signs are focused on reaching an agreement. Diplomacy and flexibility are two sides of the same coin, realized via different methodologies and strategies for each.

Libra tends to be analytical, while Pisces' heart leads the way, on a path forged by that dominant Piscean trait, intuition. Libra has trouble letting go of rationality, while Pisces has learned to trust intuition above all. This can lead to head butting. That both signs can encounter difficulties arriving at decisions further complicates the interaction between the two.

Because of the analytical side of Libra, Pisces may interpret their words and actions as emotionally detached or even cold. And while Pisces is introverted, Libra tends to be extroverted, creating potential lifestyle conflicts.

There's plenty of chemistry popping between these two, but that may show strain, eventually, as Libra takes a less serious approach to sex than Pisces, who requires an emotional and spiritual sexual connection.

If both partners are committed to understanding the needs of the other, this pairing can endure. But that commitment is necessary for the relationship to stand the test of time.

Scorpio (October 23-November 22)

This powerful, dynamic sign is so full of fire, people often believe it couldn't possibly be a water sign, but like Pisces and Cancer, that's exactly what Scorpio is.

And when Pisces gets together with Scorpio, the phrase "a match made in heaven" comes to mind. Equivalent to a pairing with Cancer, there is no match more perfect for the romantic fish than Scorpio. Reading each other's minds, this is the match that Pisces prays for.

Scorpio is committed, by nature, to protecting those nearest and dearest to them. They're leaders who apply their leadership skills to relationships, but not in a dictatorial way. They seek to make sure that no harm comes to those they love most, and for Pisces, this is a stellar trait in a partner. Scorpio, like Pisces, can intuit the motivations of others, tempering Pisces' trusting nature with an ability to identify red flags in other people.

But Pisces needs to be patient with the level of sensitivity modeled by Scorpio. This can border on paranoia. Pisces can draw Scorpio out, allowing somewhat moody Scorpio to open up and share.

There is a distinct aura to this relationship. Cocooned together, these two water signs are a mystery to others, but Pisces and Scorpio find in each other the epitome of normality. Other people are weird!

For this coupling, sex is transcendent. Meeting each other's unspoken needs by telepathy, the Pisces-Scorpio romantic couple transcends what most people think of as love. This astrological combination is intensely spiritual, going far beyond the mundane.

Sagittarius (November 22-December 21)

Represented by the archer, Sagittarius aims its bow at adventure and knowledge. This sign is dedicated to adventures of all kinds, whether travel, intellectual or spiritual.

A roadblock in the success of a relationship with a Pisces-Sagittarius couple is the direct, unfiltered nature of the archer. Sensitive Pisces isn't the biggest fan of that characteristic. It's also of note that Sagittarius gets things done, whereas Pisces needs to dream about actions before undertaking them. While this may seem lazy, this aspect of Pisces is more about envisioning the road forward than not wanting to move. Sagittarius' decisive and active nature can feel a little vulgar to the fish.

For all the hippie-dippy vibes of Pisces, people born under this sign are, by nature, conservative. Pisces thinks before speaking and looks before leaping. Not so Sagittarius. They are impulsive, appearing wild and reckless to the careful Piscean.

The Sagittarian's intensely social nature is also alien to Pisces, who desires the cocoon more than the social whirl. Sagittarius is often also non-committal about romantic relationships, which the Pisces will invariably read as an insult.

While the physical attraction between Pisces and Sagittarius can be powerful, Pisces will feel the absence of an emotional or spiritual component. Sagittarius thinks of sex in very physical terms, which can be frustrating for Pisces, for whom sex is almost a sacrament.

While this relationship can have a chance under the right conditions—mutual attentiveness being indispensable—Sagittarius is not the best match for Pisces.

Capricorn (December 22-January 19)

While Capricorn is an earth sign, they're represented by the sea-goat. This mythical creature has a tail, so it finds itself at home in both the realm of emotion and that of the material, tangible world.

Solid, practical Capricorn is an excellent complement to the emotional, mystical nature of Pisces, bringing the fish back to reality with patience, understanding, and deep love. These two find common ground with ease.

Capricorn brings romantic Pisces needed stability. With the sea-goat able to move between the realms of the material and the far-off ethers, Pisces find quiet strength in a Capricorn lover. And Capricorn, not being that affected by romantic notions, finds in a Pisces a doorway to this world of emotion and spirituality, allowing them to step into a world they sometimes shy away from.

A potential conflict between these two is money. Capricorn is keenly aware of practical, real-world concerns, while Pisces is more likely to be less than concerned with this aspect of life. This can be frustrating for both parties, with Capricorn skittish about the Piscean tendency to generosity and charity and Pisces inhibited in this respect by the care taken around money by the sea-goat.

Sexually, Capricorn loves the fun aspect of sex, entering into this side of the relationship with gusto. Pisces will love this, adding romanticism and an emotional constancy that Capricorn finds reassuring. This pairing has a great chance to succeed because of the balance between the two signs.

Aquarius (January 20-February 18)

The water bearer is an air sign which replenishes the earth, creating abundant life. Great humanist thinkers, Aquarius' most pressing concern is to mend what's broken and to heal what's hurting.

Pisces and Aquarius have little to recommend them as a match. However, Pisces' willingness to compromise may serve any relationship pursued between the two. And if Pisces can get Aquarius out of the realm of intellect that is its natural home, the two may make their pairing work.

Pisces is drawn to the intellectual nature of Aquarius, finding an outlet for its own intellectual nature, which strongly trends toward the metaphysical—an interest that many Aquarians are likely to share.

Ultimately, the cool detachment of Aquarius will puzzle a Pisces, and frustrate the fish's need for intimacy. Aquarius's many distractions and preoccupation will drive Pisces nuts, as there may seem to be no time to be fully present for the active, inquisitive Aquarian. Pisces may also feel that they're being put last, as Aquarius often gets caught up in the many interests that attract people born under this sign to the detriment of all else, including their partners.

Pisces will also have difficulty maintaining a strong connection with the water bearer, sexually. Aquarians, while adventurous and inventive lovers, will seem too detached and physically oriented to Pisces. For this reason, Pisces may wind up feeling unsatisfied with their failure to connect emotionally with Aquarius.

Pisces (February 19-March 20)

As we have learned earlier in this book, Pisces are the realization of all the 11 other signs of the zodiac's lessons. Intensely spiritual and emotional, Pisces lives. in a tension between the fantastic and the concrete.

It may seem so at first but, two fish joined in a romantic union is not a walk in the park. With two of these dreamy romantics locked in a loving embrace, the going can get a little weird.

The most dangerous aspect of a Pisces-Pisces relationship is the tendency of the two to become completely lost in each other, to the detriment of all else. The emotional tendencies of Pisces are magnified when there are two in a relationship. That can lead to severe negativity, as they feed off one another in a toxic loop.

However, if one or both Pisces in the relationship has a moon in an earth sign, there is greater hope of a successful match. With the moon being (arguably) as important as the sun in any sign, Pisces gains need stability, feet planted on the earth as they explore the ethers.

Sex for a Pisces dual coupling is almost supernatural, with the intuition of the two leading to erotic transcendence well beyond what most couples experience.

While this relationship can work, both parties should take the time to explore their respective charts before they become intimate. Two Pisces can live lives of harmonious bliss when the planets are well aligned.

Because we've discussed romantic relationships in this chapter, next, we should delve into the more complex aspects of astrology to understand how the planets in individual charts might affect the character of Pisces. As I've mentioned, the moon is a particularly strong influence that should be considered, as it's right up there with the sun. We'll also be looking into decanates to gain a more well-rounded understanding of what makes Pisces tick.

Chapter Six: Going Deeper into the World of Astrology to Understand Pisces

Many people are skeptical about astrology because its public representation is shallow. Many people believe that the sun sign determines the overall character of the zodiac.

This is a very superficial understanding of what makes astrology tick. While the sun is determined by the date of birth, other aspects of the signs are determined by far more subtle indicators, including the position of other planets in the birth chart.

While we've covered the aspects of astrology from this deeper method of inquiry in Chapter One, essential to understanding the meaning of any sign is a knowledge of other influences present during birth. So, it's not merely the date on which you were born that counts. Knowing where all the other planets were at the exact time of your birth is essential to gaining a more accurate picture of those born under the various signs.

First, let's discuss the decanates, also called "decans" in astrological circles.

A Matter of Degree

But isn't degree everything? A few inches this way, a few inches that way, and everything not only feels but looks different.

Astrology is simply a dynamic discipline of reading the movement of the planets during the specific timeframes that we were born under. This can be refined further by knowing the time. Because planets don't just swish around the solar system willy-nilly, their positions vary by degrees.

Before we move into a discussion of decans, let's get a handle on triplicities.

Every zodiac sign is ruled by one of the four physical elements—earth, air, water, and fire:

- Earth: Capricorn, Taurus, Virgo
- Air: Gemini, Libra, Aquarius
- Water: Cancer, Scorpio, Pisces
- Fire: Aries, Leo, Sagittarius

It's easy to see why these groupings are referred to as *triplicities*, with three signs in each of the four elements.

As the subtitle suggests, decans concern degrees—specifically, degrees in multiples of ten. In each sign, there are three decans, representing ten degrees each. Each of these decans, in turn, is governed by the movements of a specific planet. This is a powerful influence on people born under any sign in the zodiac. The planet your decan is ruled by is as influential as the sun sign itself. But the deeper you go into astrology, the more extraordinarily specific you'll find it is.

The first decan is a part of the same triplicity in the element of the sign in question. For example, the first decan of a planet appearing in Pisces applies to the first decan or ten degrees. This indicates the most undiluted expression of the traits for which Pisces is best known. It's the same story for all the signs.

Let's take a detailed look at the decans of Pisces. Once we understand the planetary influences on Pisces from this standpoint, it will give us a more developed picture.

February 19-February 29, First Decanate, Pisces-Pisces

In this decan (NB: the terms are interchangeable and refer to the same three ten-degree sections of Pisces), Neptune is the planetary influence, making people born during this decan double Pisces, as it is also the planet governing the sign, as a whole.

This the decan of imagination and intuition. Pisceans born in this decan can practically read your mind and predict what you'll do in any situation. These fish will also have lives full of change and adventure.

Double Pisces will have many lovers. Passionate and sensual, this variety of Pisces wants to experience everything there is to know the meaning of life better. At the heart of their explorations is spirituality. Who they click with is usually someone of tremendous energy, with superior communication skills. Pisces-Pisces also wants to know that their lovers believe in healthy living.

Double Pisces are loyal lovers who need a little nudge to pitch in, but once that nudge is received, they're in for the long haul.

Because this Pisces demands the pursuit of a healthy lifestyle, these fish will not look their age. Their health contributes to their need to explore and experience life to the fullest.

Pisces-Pisces is also driven by philanthropy and service to their community. Humility is a hallmark of this decanate, as is self-sacrifice for the good of others. Pisceans were born to be caretakers, not just those who raise children, but to care for anyone who comes into their lives.

March 01-10, Second Decanate, Pisces-Cancer

Ruled by the moon, people in this decanate enjoy the combined influences of Neptune and the warm, comforting moon. Those born in this position have a distinct sensitivity to the needs and emotions of others.

This is where you'll find Pisces at its most balanced, emotionally. In collaboration with Cancer and its ruling planet, fish in these ten degrees of their sign has a sense of humor that keeps people rolling on the floor. Wacky and eccentric, these Pisceans always have a far-out creative idea to share. You'll say it's nuts, and then you'll see that someone else made it happen decades later. Do not laugh at these unusual but brilliant people!

For the Pisces-Cancer, love is all. It transports and transforms them, satisfying their romantic natures. And the moonstruck Pisces-Cancer adores all things beautiful, from other humans to art to nature. They'll find common ground with others who take note of the details, while most miss them in the rush of life.

But this decanate is anything but lonely when alone. Comfortable in their skins and in their own company, they cherish their quiet times of solitude. Anyone wanting to get to know this special slice of Pisces will need to understand this aspect of the Pisces-Cancer.

Lest you think that Pisces-Cancer is a navel-gazing hippie, understand that these people are observers of all they see. Transformative thinkers, they build better mousetraps.

While not being particularly extroverted, Pisces-Cancers' natural charm endears them to others. Quick-witted, they're engaging conversationalists. They're also by nature obliged to be ingenious and creative.

Pisces-Cancer is the Piscean who proclaims, "Don't dream it, be it!" because that's what they do best. When their destiny rears up, they're swept forward by it, almost in the blink of an eye.

March 11-March 20, Third Decanate, Pisces-Scorpio

Ruled by the forceful, "get er' done" planet, Mars, Pisces in the third decanate satisfy the Piscean need to work off the steam that can build up in them. Because this is the last decanate in the zodiac's last sign, these Pisces are forces of nature. The momentum provided by the astrological cycle rebooting in adjacent Aries is powerful, making these Pisces dynamic information processors. Like soft computers, they suck up the data, spitting it out in a creative action once they've analyzed the input.

Love is the word that matters most to Pisces-Scorpio people. It motivates their actions and drives their decisions. Understanding those around them almost uncannily, they are the empaths.

While this sign is very expressive with their views and opinions, they are also passionate listeners. Pisceans have a remarkable talent to interpret the fundamental meanings behind other people's opinions and therefore accept them.

Pisces-Scorpio needs to feel they matter, and anyone who can do this for them will find a deep and abiding connection with this love-focused iteration of Pisces. Sensual and with a great appreciation of comfort, Pisces-Scorpio takes domestic bliss to a whole new level. If people were hugs, it would be these people.

Third decanate Pisces are visionaries, with a strong orientation toward the practical. They're often gifted in science and technology. But mostly, these folks just want to give of themselves wherever they discern a need.

Fate is more active in the lives of Pisces-Scorpio than planning. They know that the best-laid plans can go to pot in a heartbeat and so they answer the calls of life as they come, often journeying to places others would never imagine, intellectually, spiritually, and physically. Adventurers of the mind, spirit, and body, third decanate Pisceans don't suffer from the fear other mortals do. They've been there and done that. All of it.

Next, I'd like to guide you through a discussion of the moon's influence on Pisces (beyond the second decan) and how it can create an interesting synergy and a rather different breed of what we believe is the stereotypical Pisces.

How About That Moon?

As everyone reading knows, astrological skeptics abound. You know them. I know them. One of their principal beef is the claim that they're nothing like what their sun sign claims they're supposed to be like.

And that is an argument from ignorance. As I've been hinting throughout and stating clearly here and there, astrology isn't only concerned with the dates between which you were born. As we've just read in the discussion of the decans, the influence of elemental planets is a matter of degree, and a factor that makes a tremendous difference. So, we've already busted the myth.

The trouble with astrology is not that it deals in generalizations, but that people who don't understand it make generalizations about it. For many of us, that contingent bases its understanding on the popular conception of astrology, which is often considered nonsense that can be found in a newspaper column.

But when you take an interest in astrology, it rapidly becomes apparent that there's a lot more to it than two dates on the calendar. The day of your birth is as crucial to a deeper understanding and then the time of your birth.

It's the time of your birth that can produce a natal astrological chart, revealing the position of all the other signs at the moment you were born, as represented by planets. And, of all those planets, the moon is one of the most important.

It's often said in astrological circles that the moon is more influential on some people. Not knowing what moon you've been under can lead to apparent anomalies like a Taurus hula hoop artist or a Piscean chartered accountant. These are the people who will tell you, "Astrology isn't accurate! I'm the complete opposite of my sign!"

Because they're more influenced by the moon under which they were born.

While your sun sign influences external features of you as a person, like personality, the moon is what rules in the inner you. This is the part of you that's less overt and perhaps even, secret. The subconscious is ruled by the moon, for example.

Your less obvious but possibly more personally important traits and features are in the province of the moon. Only shining by night, the moon can tell us a lot about ourselves. It's simply more subtle, perhaps, than the sun.

Interestingly enough, is to think of the sun as active and the moon as reactive, reflecting back the light of the sun. Your moon sign, then, is concerned with your emotional response to the world around you.

Let's explore the influence of the moon on Pisces, occurring under the various signs. Remember, to discover your moon you must know your time of birth.

Moon in Aries

The ram paws the ground, snorting through its nostrils, head down. Likely to pick a fight when cornered, Aries wants what it wants, and charges forward to get it. They love thrills, chills, and winning. The Pisces with a moon in Aries is less likely to pass up opportunities and is markedly more extroverted than introverted.

Moon in Taurus

Slow and steady wins the race, with the patient, stable bull. When a Pisceans moon is in Taurus, they will benefit from an emotional equilibrium, and the strength to achieve their objectives in life.

Because Taurus is another lover of beauty, Pisceans with their Moon in this sign will create beauty in whatever medium they choose.

Moon in Gemini

Pisces are emotional as a way of life. Others prefer to contain their emotions as a private matter. With Moon in Gemini, Pisces is demonstrative and forthcoming about their feelings at any moment and in any setting. This is a Gemini trait, as this sign values emotional openness.

Moon in Cancer

Since both signs are water elements, the Pisces with the moon in Cancer is what some individuals would classify as psychic. They know what you're thinking, what you're planning, and what motivates others to behave the way they do. Pisces with this lunar influence need to take special care to find time away from others to clear out all the emotional flotsam and jetsam they accumulate on their travels.

Moon in Leo

When artistic Pisces is born with a moon in Leo, expect fireworks – the good kind. This is a creative dynamo, destined to ascend the heights of creative achievement. Expressive and demonstrative, this drama queen creates artistic excellence.

Moon in Virgo

This is a difficult moon for a Piscean to be born under the influence of. Virgo's incessant ambition and focus on achievement can leave emotional Pisces feeling alone. Pisceans under this moon need to be more in touch with themselves, which may require serious internal work. That way, they can wrangle the conflicts inherent in this lunar influence and be at their best. Self-knowledge is crucial.

Moon in Libra

Because relationships matter to Pisces people as much as they do to balanced Librans, Pisces with the moon in Libra may wear themselves out trying to give everything they have to their partner.

Pisceans under a Libra moon will often find they need to be open and honest with their potential partners about their expectations in a relationship. They will want to explain their acceptable behaviors, boundaries, and deal-breakers.

Moon in Sagittarius

Pisceans with their moon in Sagittarius will be hungry for knowledge and adventure. They will be passionate about seeing all the world offers and discovering anything beyond what is considered "normal." Pisces absorb the world, and with this moon, they're like super-absorbent sponges. This is Pisces unleashed, adventuring through life with gusto.

Moon in Capricorn

Industrious Capricorn gets Pisces rooted in reality and the need to do the work to get to their dreams. When influencing dreamy, esoteric Pisces, the effect is startling. Pisces are at their most creatively productive and potent with their moon in Capricorn. The only concern is the tendency to work themselves to death, instead of attending to other needs and priorities in a balanced way.

Moon in Aquarius

A Pisces whose moon is in Aquarius is actively engaged in doing good for humanity. This is the influence of Aquarius, which is most noble, and, when taken up by the empathic Pisces, it becomes a movement unto itself. With Pisces' creativity and innovative thinking, this lunar influence is extremely dynamic.

Moon in Pisces

This is the Old Soul's Old Soul. People born under both the sun and moon of this sign will often find the world a rude place to be, with their otherworldly, spiritually intense natures. But when this archetypal, almost totemic Pisces understands what he or she is sitting on and knows how to deploy it, expect magic.

I hope everyone reading is beginning to get a feel for the intricate, multi-faceted discipline that astrology is. Anything but superficial, I hope that people approach it with respect. It has much to reveal to us about our motivations, emotional and psychological landscapes if only we approach it with an open and respectful mind.

In our next chapter, we'll be talking briefly about astrology and biological sex. While clear that men and women are all made of the same cloth, the way we are raised, and the biological truth of who we are affects how we express those traits associated with our astrological charts.

But before you roll your eyes at me, let me just give you a hint – biological sex makes little difference beyond socially mandated assumptions about what sex means and the individual's acceptance of those assumptions as gospel. Let's talk about a 21st Century approach to astrology, which leaves behind the specter of gendered assumptions about biological sex.

Chapter Seven: What Does Sex Have To Do With Astrology?

Despite the public discourse on cerebral differences between human males and human females, I'm here to tell you there is only one kind of brain.

That brain is human. Its capabilities are not defined by biological sex. Nor is a preference for pink or blue trucks or Barbie dolls. That said, every cell in our bodies is permeated by the chemical cocktails associated with our respective sexes. Those cocktails do not affect the quality of this brain or its innate intellectual value.

So, no. Women are not from Venus. Men are not from Mars. We're all earthly creatures, and our biological sex is just one means by which we're identified by other people and one factor governing our interactions with and experience of the world.

Despite what folks tell you, the majority of the perceived differences between men and women, intellectually, are imposed by social structures and long-accepted stereotypes which have no meaning, other than to define what we, in our sexed bodies, are designed to do. These structures and stereotypes have represented, for millennia, a straitjacket demanding that humans find their place within certain societally prescribed parameters of behavior, appearance, and purpose.

All the signs of the zodiac are sexed, male or female. But let's consider the times in which astrology was established as a discipline.

A Little History for You

In Croatia, in 2012, the oldest known astrologer's board, used to provide personalized horoscopes, was discovered. The board depicted three sun signs, namely Cancer, Gemini, and Pisces.

Said to be over 2,000 years old, the board comes late to the astrology party, which started in the Ancient Near East, specifically, Babylonia. But even Babylon isn't far enough back.

The history of humans looking to the stars to guide their decision-making process and to make sense of their lives is estimated to be as old as 25,000 years.

It was in the Neolithic period that people began to understand the cyclical nature of the world, including the heavens above. Relying on these events to predict the outcomes in both agriculture and weather anomalies.

But astrology as a discipline did not take a form recognizable to us today until about 3,000 BCE in Mesopotamia. But it would be another 1,000 years until early astrology came to be the sophisticated discipline we know in modern times.

That's a long time ago, and if we understand the position of women in the Ancient Near East at about this time, we might have a better understanding of why the signs of the zodiac are sexed.

Women, once seen as religious leaders in society, have always been defined by their reproductive capacity and have been defined as the pillar of the home and the source of life. Because of this, women have been relegated to a divergent status and deemed as having less value than men. Men went to war. Men worked in physical labor.

Men led societies. Men did things outside the home. Women did things inside the home, especially raising children.

In many societies, the earliest theories of what the sexes propose have endured even until the present day. And those ideas are no more potently expressed than in astrological signs sexed either male or female.

To see what I mean, let's look at the zodiac through the eyes of biological sex and see if we can't detect the enduring themes.

> • Sexed male: Aries, Gemini, Leo, Libra, Sagittarius, and Aquarius
>
> • Sexed female: Taurus, Cancer, Virgo, Scorpio, Capricorn, and Pisces

Applying the knowledge we've gained in our discussion about the influence of the planets ruling decans and the influence of the moons of various signs, it's not difficult to see what's going on here. The signs sexed male are extroverted, while the signs sexed female are introverted. The masculine signs are aggressive, while the feminine signs are peaceful. The male signs tend to action, while the female signs tend to passivity.

Are all these claims about the signs not rooted in stereotypes about male and female roles in society?

And, if we take astrology seriously, understanding the nuanced meanings attributed to signs in all our respective charts, then are these socially constructed assumptions of any actual value?

This is controversial, but I will answer that question with an unequivocal "no." While there may be physical distinctions between male and female brains primarily concerned with brain size, corroborating with general size differentiation between men and women, there is no distinction between brain quality or capability.

Confirmed through significant research – information not accessible to the inventors of astrology in the Ancient Near East. Specifically, Gina Rippon's book, The Gendered Brain, has dismantled the assumption that "gender," which asserts that males and females have specific roles and behaviors expected of them, has anything to do with biological sex.

Rippon's work as a neuroscientist led to an intensive study of the human brain, seeking out potential differences in male and female examples. What she discovered – size, related to the broad differentials found in male and female bodies, is the sole difference. Otherwise, our brains have the same potentialities, regardless of the sex of the body in which they're found.

Why am I telling you all this? Because I am of the firm opinion that the only differences between males and females regarding astrology are the same stereotypes and other social constructs associated with a biological sex–now debunked and considered the products of earlier, less scientifically sophisticated times.

And that is why I have not included a discussion of sex differences in this book. Any sex discrepancies between men and women, and their respective behaviors, result directly from socialization as to the meaning of biological sex and not its inherent operative value.

If modern astrology is to be taken seriously it must, like all other disciplines, be developed. The components of the practice, which indicate that it embraces the beliefs of the past, must be shed. The gendered astrological sign is surely at the extreme edge of its usefulness in the 21st Century.

Not all women are passive. Not all men are aggressive. Not all males drive action in their contexts. Many women do exactly that.

The stereotypes of the past have been debunked and now is the time for astrology to acknowledge this. You may think this is arcane, but astrology is enjoying a renaissance right now and has been since about 2017. In fact, the discipline has not been as popular since the 1970s.

Perhaps it is time for astrology to evolve and finally become a comprehensive discipline rooted in the real actions of the cosmos. Would that not enhance their influence by confirming its understanding of humans beyond that achieved by the Ancients?

To illustrate further what I'm trying to share with you, let's look at what is considered the most masculine sign in the zodiac – Leo - and how two women, one globally famous and the other an acquaintance of mine, live out their roles as not kings but queens of the jungle. Recognized as the most feminine sign, we will do the same exercise with Pisces.

Queen of the Literary Jungle, J.K. Rowling

Author of the best-selling literary series in history and the only person to become a billionaire from writing, J.K. Rowling is a Leo and a woman. Not only does she fully model all the traits of the sign, but she also does so in an uncompromising, socially engaged, and philanthropic way.

She is no longer a billionaire. That's not because she blew her billions on private planes and other extravagances or because she made poor investment choices – she gave the money away.

Facing a tremendous challenge from supporters of the gender identity lobby, she has shown grace under pressure, while still producing literary works for both children and adults.

Unlike many authors whose books become films, J.K. Rowling has maintained an iron grip on her content, having creative control and right of approval on all scripts. It doesn't get much more Leo than that. It is not commonplace for an author to be given that much distinction in the production of films based on their work.

Beyond that, J.K. Rowling clawed her way to global literary success. She was on social assistance and a single mother and was a survivor of domestic abuse and sexual assault when she wrote the first of the Harry Potter books. Not only that, but she was also rejected by at least a dozen publishing houses before finding her success story.

But like a typical Leo, she didn't even blink. She knew what she had, and she kept sending it to publishers until one of them saw the value of her work. Leo doesn't give up. Leo doesn't give in, and Leo takes on all challengers, without hesitation.

Rowling is a perfect example of gender missing the mark for defining the signs of the zodiac and the characteristics of those born under them. She's lived the life far too many women are consigned to, emerging not only prosperous but victorious and gracious in her prosperity.

Money! Rosalind

Many years ago, I had a rather extraordinary Leo friend. Rosalind was a professional dancer, among other things. But the most extraordinary thing about her was the force of her personality and its effect on other people.

She insisted on being in the spotlight. It didn't matter whether she was dancing, singing, acting, or teaching; she was a force of nature and one you could not ignore. If you were lucky enough to share the stage with Rosalind, or even be in the same room with her, you were there only to bask in her glory.

Rosalind was a brand unto herself. When you said her name, most people smiled, but a few made a face. Others, who were challenged by her fame and fortune, would find themselves on her bad side.

Rosalind was not to be challenged about money under any circumstances. She collected it, eschewing the formal banking system for rolls of large denomination bills she hid all over her house.

By sheer force of her personality, and her status as an entertainer-people served her in many ways. Rosalind had an entourage behind her, from professional chefs, assistants, even a masseuse for her every desire.

Unlike Rowling, Rosalind was disinterested in any charitable endeavor from which she did not directly benefit. Male or female, the enduring love for money is a human trait, not a sexed trait. Both sexes can be as greedy, egotistical, and self-interested as the other, and Rosalind made that clear to all who knew her.

Personality is not governed by gender; it is formed by the lives we lead. And these two Leos are great examples of modeling the sign's propensity for the spotlight – one positively and one somewhat negatively. Both women described have achieved incredible heights in their careers and incredible fiscal returns. But they have done so in different ways, in a different spirit, and with a different agenda.

They're both still women, but they are classical Leos.

Now let's meet two male Pisces to challenge the sexed zodiac of the Ancients further.

The Fish Goes to Washington

People don't tend to peg Pisceans as leaders. It's a feminine sign, right? And leadership is inherently masculine! Not just that, but aren't Pisces supposed to "introverted" and "feminine"?

Well, here's a factoid for you, four US Presidents have been Pisceans. Also, in the Oval Office were James Madison, Andrew Jackson, and Grover Cleveland. Of their number, George Washington was a first decanate Pisces, with the other three being born in the second decanate.

Tell me that's not intriguing! The Pisces-Cancer decan is the segment in which transformative thinking and leadership are probably most powerful.

Putting aside the fact these were men of their times, with all the attendant prejudices one might expect, it's especially interesting to consider that two of the Founding Fathers of our nation were Pisceans. Leading people toward that more "perfect union" mentioned in our Constitution's preamble is not as strange a Piscean occupation as it seems at first glance. Without a doubt, both Washington and Madison were idealistic leaders with a compelling belief in the blooming experiment of their fledgling nation.

And then there's Andrew Jackson. Not remembered as the most sensitive or empathic leader, he is known for his infamous policy of removing Native Americans from their traditional territories, giving rise to the shameful Trail of Tears.

Again, it's important to remember the times and imperatives these presidents lived in and with. All the same, let's just admit this policy of the Jackson administration sucked and certainly doesn't sound like something a Pisces would sign off on.

As for Grover Cleveland, he was the last Pisces to be President, and he did so in two non-consecutive terms in office, as the 22nd and 24th President. Widely admired, even by his fellow GOP at the time, Cleveland was an enemy of corruption and a champion of honesty and integrity.

The 20th and 21st Centuries have deprived the USA of Piscean leadership, but it's hoped that a little of that Pisces magic will make its way back to the White House at an opportune time.

My Cousin, Bob

Bob is not discernable as a Pisces to any but his nearest and dearest. Gruff and disinterested in philosophy, religion, the meaning of life, or basically anything except sports, he would seem to be your typical redneck.

Bob is always right, even when he's wrong. Bob will fight you over a perceived slight, faster than you can blink. Bob is always demanding apologies for those perceived slights. I have not spoken to Bob for almost five years, and it's unlikely that I will again.

As a kid, Bob was fond of attacking me with a variety of weapons, from ballpoint pens to his fingernails, which he kept long for precisely that purpose. When I saw my cousins pulling up to our front door, I knew that I'd have a few scars at the conclusion of the visit.

The most Piscean trait of Bob is his raw, almost self-pitying sensitivity. Like an open wound, the slightest glance can set him off on a rant about what a horrible person you are. Going back to his childhood again, Bob was known for soaring tantrums, which featured physical feats of strength like levitation. On all fours, Bob could get daylight as he pounded the floor with his fists and knees.

I don't know of any neurological reasons for Bob's personality. He is just Bob, and that's the way it has always been. Why is Bob like this? Bob is like this because, at his root, he is a sensitive child who demands you respect him, his authority, his grudges, and his insistence on apologies for things that may or may not have happened.

Permanently set to "disgruntled," the only aspect of Bob, which is even vaguely Piscean, is his pathological sensitivity. Incurious as the day is long, Bob is content to drink beer in front of the TV when he's not driving a rig.

So, not only is Bob the least inquisitive, dreamy Pisces I've ever met, he is also the only redneck, trucker hat and flannel-shirt-wearing Pisces I believe to exist.

So, four US Presidents and a truculent, hypersensitive redneck – all of whom were and are Pisceans. All are men. And they all represent something of a departure from what we anticipate from the supposedly "feminine" Pisces.

While a few may continue to disagree, assigning sex to a zodiac sign in recognition of gendered assumptions about men and women- only confuses the discipline of astrology further.

With our knowledge today about dimorphic, biological sex – which is that all people have personalities and experiences which guide their actions and choices in life – it's risky to believe in the notion that masculinity and femininity have anything at all to do with astrology. Whether we're accepting the sexing of the signs of the zodiac by the ancient founders of the discipline, or claiming that men and women live out the traits of their zodiac signs differently, I continue to assert that it is time to let those old beliefs go.

As we stand on the cusp of the Age of Aquarius - rumored by astrologers to begin on December 01, 2020 - perhaps this is a project whose time has come. As we transition from the Age of Pisces, during which Age monotheistic religion and philosophy rooted in the same gendered assumptions and too often guided by them arose, maybe this is an opportunity for the astrological community to lead.

As I've said throughout this exploration of Pisces, so many factors affect the way you exhibit the traits of your sun sign. From the era you're born in, to your personality, to the movement of the planets in your sign, the date and time, all these factors have a strong influence on the way we model the associated traits.

But one factor is not, to my knowledge, biological sex. As we learn more about biological sex, and begin to understand that men and women are defined by this, it becomes clearer that we cannot continue the practice of sexing the zodiac. It is misleading and harmful to the deeper understanding of astrology's true work - which is in the stars, not the flesh.

A fresh start without a sexed zodiac? I'm in!

Our next chapter will explore Pisces and friendship. Who they love to hang out with, who they avoid and who they can change the world with!

Chapter Eight: Pisces Friends, Enemies, and Collaborators

Pisces, while inherently introverted, is, as I've mentioned before, semi-social. While fond of spending plenty of time at home with their nearest and dearest (especially their beloved pets), Pisces also loves to spend time with people they feel understood and appreciated by – just like everyone else! However, semi-social Pisces will need time and solitude to recharge after every foray into the world. When that's not available to the shy fish, they're liable to get a little cranky.

In this chapter, I'd like to take a walk through the zodiac to identify a few of Pisces' most likely cronies, enemies, friends, and collaborators. Synergies happen, and each synergy between people's specific application bears significant fruit, under the right circumstances.

Let's find this cast of astrological characters and see what they're most likely to do – or not do – with Pisces when they're around. My standard disclaimer applies here – rising signs (which we'll examine in the next chapter, with a deeper look at the Houses) and the planetary influences associated with them, as well as the moons, decanates, and cusps, can strenuously influence all signs. So, it's important to remember that we're all under the auspices of the planets, as they make their way through the sky.

But before we get started, know that Pisces, while shy and retiring, is also one of the best friends you'll ever have. The empathic nature of a Piscean compels them to be the shoulder to cry on, the source of good advice, and the compassionate friend that always knows what to say.

But Pisces has needs that not everyone understands or cares about. Being sensitive and emotionally driven, this sun sign relates best with the other sun signs, which understand them on a deeper level. Let's find out who Pisces really clicks with, becoming fast friends for life.

Best Friends Forever

Pisces are sensitive, not just to the things people around them say and do. They're sensitive to social and emotional undercurrents like no other sign. Arch-empaths, they possess a unique quality to sense the emotional landscapes of other people. This is both a blessing and a curse because being in large groups of people or even in conversation with one other person encountering difficult emotions can leave them drained.

For this reason, Pisces needs to know that they can trust their friends implicitly. They need to be sure that their closest confidants will keep their confidences, as Pisces keeps theirs. No matter who you are, I'm sure you'll agree that people like that are few and far between. For this reason, we will take great care in choosing those around us who we associate with on a personal level.

And Pisces takes that selection process so seriously that others can interpret their reticence as coldness or snobbery. But Pisces will vet you harder than a political party's machinery will a candidate for public office. They need to be 100% convinced that their emotional investment in you will not blow up in a fiery inferno of disappointment and betrayal.

So, don't take it personally if you catch Pisces observing you from the other side of the room. They'll probably wave at you, smile, and then go back to observing you. They don't care if you notice. And once you've passed the audition, you'll find that Pisces is as loyal and nurturing a friend as you could ever hope to find.

And if you don't make it? I suppose it depends on what the issue is! If you're a bold, aggressive type, it's likely Pisces won't want to have much to do with you. They won't slam the door in your face, but they probably won't invite you inside, either.

Important to remember: Manipulation, lying, unfair gossip, character assassination, and other unfortunate social behaviors will slam that door in your face before you know it. Any hint of these behaviors under the surface of a personality can set Pisces off.

Pisces has a sixth sense for problem people, toxic people, narcissists, exploiters, and anyone else who doesn't have the best of intentions. They can smell it, and if they smell it on you, you're over. You're done. Pisces will see you coming and walk on the other side of the street. You have been warned.

Taurus

Stable, patient Taurus brings Pisces the solid friendship they long for. Strongly rooted in the real world, Taurus is practical and will serve as a great advisor to the fish.

Both signs are deeply tolerant of the foibles of others and incredibly compassionate. These two take having each other's backs to a new level. Intensely loyal, they create a bond that's founded on mutual trust and positive feedback.

Pisces helps Taurus unwind, while Taurus is likely to keep Pisces laughing. In each other's company, they don't even notice how comfortable they are with each other, as this is a given in their friendship and why they love each other too pieces.

While Pisces may find Taurus to be a little too focused on the material, Pisces will frustrate the bull with the notorious fishy forgetfulness. They get over these minor details to form a lifelong bond.

Cancer

Both these signs are water babies, so there's an immediate attraction by both to their respective similarities. Pisces and Cancer have an almost unconscious synergy, with Cancer bringing the ideas and Pisces bringing the imagination to transform them.

These two are a team who love sharing "in-jokes" and plans to improve the world around them. Both intensely emotional and connected to the collective unconscious, they see a problem and join forces to fix it, deploying their complimentary gifts.

Pisces has the insight to help Cancer learn to compromise, while Cancer has the tools to help Pisces understand that doing one thing at a time is probably more effective than doing, say, twenty!

These two are friends for life, sharing an intense loyalty and belief in the sanctity of friendship. Together, they're a force to be reckoned with.

Scorpio

A water sign like both Pisces and Cancer, Scorpio forms a bond with Pisces that's almost at a spiritual or soulmate level. While they may not become instant best friends, in discovering each other, they often will find a kindred spirit.

Scorpio's depth of thinking is highly attractive to the fish. They find in this an excellent outlet for their love of analytical thinking about the motivations of others. As Scorpio plots a course forward, Pisces rides shotgun, looking for the esoteric, hidden details Scorpio may have overlooked in the passion of the moment.

Both signs have a tendency to go inward. While this quality can be annoying to people born under other sun signs, these two forgive it in each other. They know why the other is doing it and understand that the hijinks they get up to together – which are often in the realm of personal or public politics – require that level of reflection before action.

Scorpio's extreme idealism is a good match for a Pisces friend, with Pisces smoothing off the often rough edges of the intense scorpion, intuiting the truth of the matter. Scorpio's dog, with a bone approach, when combined with the Piscean connectivity to a deeper level of reality, can achieve amazing things. This friendship is a keeper and a gift to humanity.

Capricorn

The stubborn goat finds a fast friend in compassionate Pisces, and while on the surface, this seems an odd pair, their friendship is often enduring and fruitful.

Because Pisces is so highly intuitive, the fish knows that the Capricorn's sharp elbows are just part of the package, laughing off the goat's gruff exterior. Pisces knows there's a big softie in there and then brings that aspect of Capricorn forth, with their familiar patience and love.

In fact, Pisces is in charge of this relationship managing its emotional aspects, while Capricorn puts their nose to the grindstone, achieving and accumulating the comfort this sign enjoys. Meanwhile, Capricorn reminds Pisces that the earth appreciates having the fish's feet on it occasionally.

And Pisces tempers Capricorn's gravitas by injecting an element of fancy into this serious, hardworking sign's life. There is tremendous balance in this friendship that serves both parties well.

Now that we've got a handle on Pisces' BFFs, it's time to look at the other side of the coin.

While Pisceans are easy to love and generally well-liked, not everybody can be close friends with this sun sign's denizens. Many people in our lives are a passing nod in the street or a beer at the corner bar. Others are thorns in Pisces's scaly sides, inflicting unpleasant emotions that need to be avoided at all costs. They rub the fish the wrong way, and when that's the case, Pisces will keep on swimming to get away. This next section addresses people Pisces should stay away from as much as possible.

Virgo

The virgin is someone the fish should avoid. Unless Pisces is willing to tailor themselves to the demands of this obsessive-compulsive, nitpicky, perfectionist sign, they will quickly be at odds and feel suffocated.

Rigid in their decision-making process, Virgo is unlikely to take the consultative, communal approach to life. It's their way or the highway which leaves the fish feeling unwelcome, unloved, and disrespected.

The precipitously high standards of the Virgo – a function of their obsessive perfectionism – seem unfair and unduly harsh. Virgo also tends to have very fixed ideas about what constitutes the truth and reality, while Pisces' fluidity rejects that kind of thinking.

Even with Pisces' innate flexibility, dealing with Virgo can be disorienting and soul-crushing for the sensitive fish.

Leo

The audacious, spotlight loving lion and shy Pisces are polar opposites. And while, on a distant planet, these two may somehow find common ground, on this planet, they're unlikely to get along.

The lion may find Pisces' shyness intriguing, wanting to understand it better, while the fish may admire the bombastic Leo's ability to command a room. But the disparities between their character traits can wear thin with time; familiarity has bred contempt.

Leo's monolithic ego grates on sensitive, humble Pisces. They're unable to process the continual proclamations of superiority and tales of victory, eventually identifying these as the smoke and mirrors they are.

Ultimately, the egotism and self-centered preening of Leo will drive the quiet, reflective Pisces away.

But keep reading because you're about to get a big surprise regarding Pisces and Leo. While true that these guys don't get along, pair them on a project at work or in the community, and watch the hostile sparks turn into the right kind of fireworks. These two, when working shoulder to shoulder, are quite a tasty match.

As I said a little earlier, the Pisces is hard not to like. Gregarious, while shy, entertaining, while humble, Pisceans make great friends for many people. But those people are not usually born under Virgo or Leo. As with everything else in this book, the mileage may vary. When the planets are aligned, everything you've just read can prove either untrue or partially true.

However, these two signs are bad bets for Pisces, and with the sensitive, emotional framework of Pisceans, they can prove to be highly corrosive influences. As acquaintances, you can enjoy each other's company, but pursuing an up close and personal relationship with these two signs is a bad bet for Pisces.

Next, let's have a look at the better collaborators for Pisces in the zodiac. These may not prove to be lifelong friends. They may be present in the life of the Pisces for only a brief time, teaching them important lessons and sharing a moment the relationship may have been expressly created to address.

For work, personal developments, and even political engagement, these signs are a few of Pisces' most influential and valuable collaborators.

Leo

Whether producing a charity gala or managing a project at work together, Pisces will find collaboration with a Leo like a trip to an amusement park. Leo wants to ride the gnarliest rollercoaster possible, and Pisces is coming along for the ride.

Thrills! Chills! Abject terror! These are all part of the experience when you're working alongside risk-taking Leo.

The advantage of this collaboration for Pisces is that Leo is perfectly willing to do all the heavy going, while Pisces plugs along in the background. Pisces couldn't care less about fame and fortune, while Leo lives for them, so putting the lion out front is a winning strategy for shy, reflective Pisces. An effective collaboration if ever there was one!

Libra

Light-hearted Libra is usually a good match for Pisces, on the job, or working at other projects. Libra loves a good laugh, so they'll make an entertaining company for Pisces.

Sometimes, though, Libra may seem less than engaged with the project at hand. A Piscean can learn from this; finding they need not put themselves last by constantly trying to please those around them.

And while Libra isn't the glory hound that Leo is, they do better on the front end of things than sensitive Pisces, especially if we're talking customer service or prickly clients. Libra's diplomacy covers those bases, while Pisces keeps the back end moving along as it should.

Aquarius

The philanthropic water bearer makes Pisces' best collaborator when working on humanitarian projects. Whether that's a non-profit dedicated to saving water resources or a school for children with learning disabilities, the two balance each other well.

Aquarius can facilitate the visionary prognostications of Pisces, creating a unique synergy that improves outcomes by injecting creativity into the work. With logical Aquarius at the controls, Pisces may dream their visions into being.

An emotional Pisces meets a brilliant collaborator in the logical Aquarius, joining rationality to intuition, often with exemplary results.

The discussion in this chapter is about specific signs and who they are to Pisces. Pisces natives will find there are many others out in the world they're able to form strong friendships with and work with. While people under signs they wouldn't normally find difficult can become resolute enemies.

Astrology is complex. As I've been trying to communicate throughout this book, this discipline is not as cu-and-dried as it may appear in a quarter-inch newspaper column. Planetary influences, such as the operation of the moon on your sun sign, and other key effects can change the game.

So, this is intended to share with you the more obvious personalities and their potential roles in your life. With astrology, nothing is written in stone. Just as the course of planetary motions brings continual change to the universe, it brings variety to every sign of the zodiac. This is a crucial point that should always be remembered.

In our next chapter, we'll discuss the work of rising signs and houses, what they mean and how they might affect Pisces. I've given it a chapter all its own because it's another interesting, deeper way of approaching astrology as a discipline for understanding other people and what makes them tick.

Chapter Nine: Rising Signs, Houses and What They Mean to Pisces

Before we dive in, I should make readers aware that the rising signs and Houses are other aspects of astrology for which you must know your time of birth. If you're interested, I highly recommend having your astrological chart done. This is a metaphorical choice that will help you understand yourself, and the significance of your sun sign with much more clarity. And if you have read this far, I will assume you are!

Your rising sign is also called your "ascendant." It refers to the planet associated with any given astrological sun sign, which is rising in the eastern sky at the exact time and place of your birth.

And ascendents don't refer solely to people. They also refer to events.

Interestingly, Donald Trump's rising sign is Leo. I mean, the hair, right? Never mind everything else. If only we'd done his chart right after that announcement in New York, back in the year BTD (Before The Donald). We might have noticed this Gemini ran a little hot.

What Does it All Mean?

The rising sign governs the way you look at the world, as well as your outward appearance. This is the key factor that is responsible for the first impression you make on people. So, what people see in you isn't necessarily what they'll eventually get if they stick around. It's just the surface of you and what you project.

So, let's visit the rising signs and how they manifest in the astrological chart and the lives of individuals they impact in the birth chart. Remember that what we're referring to in this chapter are general attributes and effects of the rising sign. Without a natal birth chart for everyone reading, I can't get any further than that. If you want to know – and it's important – then you must get a chart done, and to do that, you'll need your time of birth. Once you know your exact time of birth, you can get an accurate chart online at Astro.com.

While reading, remember that the attributes bestowed by ascendents will seem out of character for Pisces, but these are general attributes, having similar – but not precisely the same – impacts on all those they rise upon. Other influences in the chart will also be in play, as always.

PRO-TIP: Don't rely on mom and dad for the time of your birth. They may be a little fuzzy on that point. Instead, obtain a long-form birth certificate, as this document will give you the precise time you were born.

Aries

With Aries as your ascendant, you make quite a strong impression, with many believing you to be intimidating at the first meeting. People will initially find you to be opinionated.

Aries being both the first sign of the zodiac and a fire sign, your ascendent in Aries means you see your life and the world around you as one long competition. Impulsive Aries operates from instinct, blazing trails others can't imagine.

Taurus

Even a Pisces can seem willful and perhaps a little ferocious with a Taurus rising sign. While the ram has a softer side, you emit a warning that you are not to be messed with.

Taurus loves the finer things in life, from beautiful clothes to sumptuous home décor and haute cuisine. This can lead others to believe they're materialistic. For Taurus, seen as first earth element in the zodiac sign, what others believe is materialism is really sensuality. That's especially true for and Aries rising Pisces.

Gemini

Pisces, under the ascendant of the twins, is seen as a busy bee, undertaking multiple projects at once and facing them all. You're a bolt of lightning at work, home, and in your social group.

This rising sign creates energy in the languid fish, making Pisces the center of the creative universe, transforming ideas into reality. The only problem is the potential for burnout. Pisces with this ascendent should take care to focus on a couple of things at once to avoid that effect.

Cancer

With Cancer rising, Pisces is augmented, shifting from best friend to mother of whichever company you're part of. Your warm nature gets even warmer, taking on the characteristics of a luxuriously fuzzy blanket, ever at the ready to wrap itself around someone needing comfort.

Home, comfort, and stability are important to those with Cancer rising. You present to others as a nurturing port in the storm, or someone who is always willing to listen when a problem occurs.

Leo

Leo rising brings fire to even the fiercest of fire signs. For Pisces, the presence of this ascendant means that everyone knows when you've walked into the room. This is the sign of the presence and the eternal sun of summer, and you shine it happily on the world around you.

Leo rising can also be a little overwhelming at times, as the lion has needs. Like a baby, those needs will be met. Take care to remember you're an adult and that your friends, lovers, and workmates aren't your nannies.

Virgo

This ascendant sometimes brings "fuzzy on the details" fish the organizational skills needed to complement their creative, intuitive spirit. People also sense your immovable reliability when your rising sign is Virgo.

The earthiness of this rising sign augments Pisces' love of nature and animals and enhances a belief in the sanctity of this planet we all live on. Virgo rising transforms external perceptions of you to acknowledge a stable foundation.

Libra

The scales represent balance and equal justice, and that's reflected in a Libra rising sign by investing Pisces with the spirit of diplomacy. You're perceived as someone pleasant to be around.

While many find Libra indecisive, what's really at work is that they're trying to arrive at the best outcome for all concerned. So, perhaps the scales are more about socialism than diplomacy. Either way, this pragmatic sign needs to understand that no matter the outcome, someone will always feel unhappy. Work on accepting that.

Scorpio

Pisceans with Scorpio rising are perceived as mysterious, reticent, and attractive in every way possible. Already somewhat mysterious, Pisces becomes someone people are immediately curious about with Scorpio as their ascendant.

But you aren't all that easy to get to know. You take your time with people, vetting them as political parties might vet their potential candidates for office. You don't take chances with close relationships, which can be off-putting until people get to know you.

Sagittarius

Pisces gets a healthy dose of optimism with the sea-goat as their ascendant. Fun-loving and adventurous, Sagittarius is the explorer of the zodiac, taking you where no Pisces had gone before – unless they were Sagittarius rising!

You'll be heard saying what others are reluctant to say because you have strong opinions. This can blow up in your face if care isn't taken with the notorious Sagittarian "tell it like it is" method of communication.

Capricorn

Often equated with the sure-footed, solitary mountain goat, Capricorn rising is seen by others as dependable and mature. Ever prepared and ready for anything, they insist on excellence from themselves, as they do from others.

Capricorn's quest for achievement takes them places others fear. This ascendent removes any doubt from the sensitive Pisces soul, investing it with courage and the resolve to reach the greatest heights possible.

Aquarius

Aquarius' philanthropic intellect is a great complement to Pisces when it's your rising sign. Concerned with collective action and the communal good, the water bearer is about sharing the wealth.

Marching to the beat of your own drum, you can be intimidating, but only those who are threatened by your resolute idealism and self-confidence. While concerned with the greater good, you're every inch a head-turning individual, when Aquarius is the rising sign you're born under.

Pisces

At birth, Pisces are even odder when the rising sign is the same as their sun sign. This sign's psychic nature is richly fortified by this rising sign, making them a little difficult for others to understand.

Pisces rising Pisceans may seem as though they're on another planet to the rest. But what's actually going on is that they're collecting data and forming an analysis. This can be unnerving for many. The Pisces need be careful to keep their thoughts clear, specific to that person, and leave the mind-reading for another day.

Now that we've taken a walk through the rising signs and their significance, it's time to talk about another important aspect of astrology we discussed earlier – the Houses. As promised in Chapter One, we'll get to the heart of what the Houses mean here.

Everything floating around out in the heavens, transit the signs of the zodiac, and each is significant in your birth chart. Each of the Houses these celestial bodies transit has much to tell you about yourself.

The twelve houses of the zodiac represent sectors of your life. That said, none are isolated from the others completely. The twelve Houses comprise a 360-degree totality, symbolizing the cosmology of the individual concerned.

Again, you'll need your time, date, and location of birth to produce a chart before you can get a clear picture of Houses' impact on your chart. For the purposes of this book, I will keep this section simple. It must be known that the Houses are quite complicated in their operation, so please do further research to raise your consciousness about this subject.

What are They?

Twelve, as you may have noticed throughout this book, is a mystical number that is foundational to the discipline of astrology. This number also appears in a variety of religions, including Judaism,

Christianity, and Islam. In Judaism, particularly, numbers are invested with a deep, spiritual significance.

So, like the sun signs, there are twelve sections in your birth chart, including the twelve astrological houses.

That is not to say that the Houses are analogous to the sun signs, which are based on the annual solar rotation. The Houses are based on the rotation of the earth, which occurs every 24 hours. For accuracy, the Houses rotate on the earth's axis, necessitating the need for the time of birth.

The astrological Houses shift every four minutes, which leaves little room for error. This explains why even those born on the same day can have wildly divergent charts.

Every House stands for a different area of your life. It also reveals notable obstacles you may face in your life and the gifts you've been born to exploit. So, whatever you do, if you're genuinely interested in an accurate reading, get that time of birth and make sure it's 100% accurate by requesting a long-form birth certificate.

Reading Your Natal Chart

To accurately read your natal chart, you must adapt to a new language, and that language is governed by the Houses. To further understand it, you will need to locate your rising sign. This is the crux of the astrological chart, appearing at the radical left of the horizon line dividing the chart in half.

You know from reading this far that the sun is your truth, the moon is your inner life, and the rising sign is your public face, revealing your personality and determining the perceptions others harbor about you, as discussed earlier in this chapter.

The rising sign or ascendant is of primary importance to your chart because it determines its unique form.

Natal charts are intended to be read counterclockwise. The horizontal line of the rising sign marks the first House. Following on from there, the Houses proceed to the right side of the horizon. This takes you through all the Houses until you get to the twelfth House, which abuts your rising sign.

Many of you reading learning how to interpret your natal charts may find numerous planets in various of your Houses. Others will see no planets in a few Houses. All you're seeing is a celestial "Polaroid" of where the planets all were at the exact moment you came into the world. Their positions in your chart illuminate your personality, your life challenges, and your areas of expertise (gifts). And each House of the zodiac will manifest in your life at certain times, as the planets continually move, affecting disparate life sectors at certain times.

Next, let's go through the twelve Houses and figure out what they mean.

First House

This is the House of your appearance and how you present yourself to others. The planet in your 1st House is a powerful influence on your life. This House corresponds to the first sign in the zodiac, Aries, and impacts goals, ideas, or attitudes that are part of who you are, defining your purpose.

Second House

This House, corresponding to Taurus, governs money, the value you attach to things, and what you own. Planets in this House at your birth determine security and financial stability. Those planets are just passing through this House express changes, particularly to your self-esteem and monetary success.

Third House

Gemini's energy is infused into this House, governing your community, transportation, and matters pertaining to communication. Planets at the time of your birth in this House are concerned with the way you express yourself and the relationships you build with those around you. Planets transiting the third House bring crucial information about the people in your most intimate circles.

Fourth House

You'll find this Cancerian House located at the bottom of your chart. It's concerned with family and the home, especially with respect to domestic life. When planets are moving through this House, we're urged to take care of our personal infrastructures, re-envisioning them as more nurturing and intimate.

Fifth House

Invested with the energy of Leo, the Fifth House is all about romance, creativity, and the children in your life. This is also the House of artistic pursuits. Transiting planets bear epiphanies that lift us up and fortify our confidence.

Sixth House

This is the House of Virgo, concerned with wellness, your daily life, and health. Your lifestyle choices impact the physicality expressed in the First House, which is concerned with the body you're born with. Natal planets here govern the structure, organization, and time management. Transiting planets support us in forming good habits and intelligent scheduling.

Seventh House

The diplomacy and pragmatic gifts of Libra create the energy influencing this House, which is the descendent, located opposite the ascendent of your First House. You'll note that so far, in our discussion of astrological Houses, each House has governed a specific sector of your life. This House is more about partnerships. Here, natal planets hone in on relationships. Those planets are transiting the Seventh House influence deal-making and binding contracts.

Eighth House

Energetically infused with Scorpio's passion, the Eighth House is the sector governing transformation. Transformation, in this instance, refers to the power of both sex and death. Natal planets cleave to the unseen world and the occult. Transiting planets reveal the unseen in any situation and remind us that life is a complicated matter.

Ninth House

The Ninth House is all about education, philosophical thinking, and, of course, travel, as this is Sagittarian turf. Exploration is the name of the game for the natal planets governing this House. Curious and inquisitive, the Ninth House is the locus of the explorer. Planets transiting it encourage us to learn new things, move somewhere unknown with a tremendous leap of faith, or to change our minds about something.

Tenth House

Positioned in the constant energy of Capricorn, this house is the pinnacle of your life's heroic tale. This House is what drives your dreams and achievements and public image. The planets in the Tenth House at the time of your birth are concerned with ambition. When planets are moving through it, you may have a profound change in your professional aspirations and path.

Eleventh House

At this point in your chart, the purpose is highlighted. With Aquarian energy at the wheel, this House governs our philanthropic work and our networks, which are further away from us. Those born in this House are the innovators, bringing fresh ideas to the world. Planets moving through the Eleventh House broaden our horizons, helping us find our rightful places in the world.

Twelfth House

This is the House of what is not seen. It's shrouded in mystery just like the sun sign, which infuses it energetically, Pisces. Governing all that is formless from our emotions to our dreams to the information we keep to ourselves, planets in this House in our charts induce extreme intuition. When planets transit this House, our karma is incarnated by people suddenly appearing in it, who are connected to that karma. Important to remember: many people in our lives are just passing through.

Now that you have a grounding in the intricacies of astrology, I'm sure you're curious about your chart. All this information you've read regarding your birth chart requires that all-important time of birth. With that information in place, you're set to discover more about who you are and what you're here to do.

In our next chapter, I'd like to spend a little time on what Pisces needs and how the Piscean energy manifests in the world when those needs are met. While we can't all have every need met all the time, we can work toward the conditions which need to exist before most of them can be, most of the time.

Let's find out how Pisces can set themselves up for the kind of lives they're capable of having when they understand themselves and what they need and get proactive to that end!

Chapter Ten: What Pisces Need to Thrive

Now that you've arrived at a more well-rounded understanding of the Pisces sun sign and how astrology influences us all as humans, it's time to talk about what Pisces needs to thrive in a world that can be unkind to the sensitive people born as fish.

It's not as though there's anything wrong with them! Quite the contrary, there's plenty to love about Pisces. The problem is the sensitivity of this sign and the shyness which plagues many if not all born Pisces.

So, this chapter will explore what Pisces need to live their best lives and how they can lay the foundation to have those needs met. Much of it has to do with personal feelings, but there's a need for Pisces to make sure that they're happy where they are, in what they're doing, and *with whom* they're doing it.

Self-Acceptance

One of Pisces' greatest life challenges is accepting who they are and being in love with all that means. The reflective nature of Pisces continually prompts them to question themselves, their decisions, even to parse the words they've said to other people to make sure they haven't said the wrong thing.

Pisces also labors under something of an inferiority complex, needing the reassurance of those around them to feel confident about who they are. But what that's really about is the Pisces tendency to neurotic self-critique and self-recrimination.

Remember my Pisces friend? She told me a story once from high school about a boy in her drama club – of course, where else would Pisces be, except maybe art class or creative writing class? This boy was always in trouble. His home life was difficult, and he was a bit off the rails because of that environment, which included absentee parents with substance abuse problems. Of course, Pisces felt for this boy. While other kids at school weren't that interested in him and avoided him, lest they be tarred with the dysfunction brush, my friend became a confidante of his.

Then, one day, my friend and this guy were in the props room at the school theater and dang it, if that boy didn't knock over and smash an old, porcelain teapot to smithereens.

The boy was terrified. He'd just come off an expulsion and knew that if he were caught for damaging a prop, the teacher would have a fit. My friend knew he was right, so when the drama teacher saw the smashed teapot, asking who had been responsible for the incident, my friend bravely raised her hand.

Her impulse to protect this boy overwhelmed her common sense. She'd been one of the top students in that class and had believed the teacher would accept her version of events. But he not only knew better – he didn't like the boy.

My noble Piscean friend was called into the drama teacher's office and dressed down. She was then kicked out of the class for the remainder of her time in senior high. This crushed her, as she loved being in plays and performing, learning lines, and taking on different characters. But the teacher would not be moved. She was kicked out.

After that, she abandoned any hope of involving herself in acting or dramatic pursuits, as the hurt never healed.

Rather than allow the errant boy to own up to his mistake, my friend took on his punishment. While she never regretted preventing her friend from getting in trouble again, she always regretted losing her connection to the drama community in her school.

This is the self-sacrificial, compassionate nature of Pisces. She took on the error of her friend, taking a fall that wasn't hers to take. And that's a serious problem. Unfortunately, one of the most pressing needs of Pisces is to believe that they are worthy of love, kindness, and compassion. Because Pisces is so deeply self-critical, many of its denizens struggle with self-acceptance. That failing can lead to acts like the one I've just described to you. Noble, yes. Smart? No.

This is why Pisceans need cheerleaders who tell them when they've done something right, that reminds them that they're good people with good intentions and worthy of all the compassion they show others. Pisces needs to understand that compassion for the self is the root of all other compassion. When it's not, Pisces can become cranky. All they need to do to fix their compassion fatigue is to apply that trait to themselves.

Friends Willing to Listen and Advise

Another pressing need for Pisces is to attract friends who will listen to Pisces as much as Pisces will listen to them.

While Pisces is happy to dispense the advice and wisdom others come to them for, it's often the case that when Pisces needs a should to cry on, it's not there. This nurturing sign is the agony aunt of the zodiac, but mothers everywhere will tell you they have the same problem as Pisces; people don't believe they need that support.

The kindness and embrace of the fish are sought out by all who know them. It's often the case, though, that no one's around when Pisces needs those gifts reciprocated. The otherworldly aura of spiritual intelligence associated with Pisces often misleads people into believing that they'll figure it out on their own - and that they're emotionally superhuman.

But fish are people, too! Pisceans need the listening ear and the sympathetic voice of caring reason as much as anyone else does. Despite their status as Old Souls who've been around the block many times, Pisces is a highly sensitive star sign. The Piscean needs to know there are people who will be there in their time of need.

This can be a huge challenge for Pisces, as many in their lives will misunderstand them. Often, Pisceans find themselves cast as flighty, out-to-lunch, and hippie-dippy. While this is true to an extent, those who do not have an open mind are missing out on the wellspring of beauty the Pisces can bring to their lives.

Their love is endless, but it's easily bruised when these delicate creatures are not treated with the tender hands they need to be well in their scaly skins. That is a problem, both for Pisces and those in their personal and professional circles.

A Piscean rejected, rebuffed, humiliated, or slighted is likely to hold a grudge. That grudge can endure until the Apocalypse if you don't clear things up with your sensitive, watery friend. You're likely to find that your phone number has been permanently lost and that you're blocked on every conceivable social media channel.

Because Pisces only gives second chances to those who ask for them. If you're walking around with your head up your backside, wondering why your Pisces friend no longer speaks to you, you're probably far too insensitive a person to be in the company of Pisces. They won't be calling any time again soon – or unblocking you!

Creative Outlets

Another key need for Pisces is an outlet for the boundless creativity of the sign. That creativity may take many shapes, from painting to sculpture to embroidery to writing to engineering to pottery to politics to dance. These guys have bright ideas about how anything you name can be improved with a dose of creative thinking.

Without a locus for their endless ideas and inspirations, Pisces can become stagnant, resentful, and even depressed. That's why it's so important that they don't just work for its own sake. While we all need to work to make a living and support ourselves, Pisces needs to find their way into work situations that give them opportunities to let their creativity shine.

And that can mean just about anything. What it doesn't mean is working at a job that's repetitive and mundane that the Pisces turns off. This is often the reason that Pisceans, especially young Pisceans, can seem lazy in the wrong environment, leading to them losing job after job.

The same is true of Pisces at home. Television isn't enough for these folks. While they'll thrill to the design genius and exceptional writing of shows like *Mad Men* and *Ratched,* they die a little inside when all their partner wants to do at night is a slouch on the couch in front of the idiot box.

Pisces would rather scribble down a great idea, refinishing a piece of furniture, or painting a mural on the living room wall, then being crushed under the mundane weight of mass media, any day. That's important for people who partnered with Pisces to remember. A bored Pisces is a listless, uninspired Pisces who is likely to bolt.

Besides work and the home, Pisces needs to seek inspiration. Curious and exploratory, Pisces loves to learn something new or interesting. Whatever their passions are, they need to have an outlet to their inner genius, and to share it with others similarly connected. Whether that's being part of a committee to beautify their town, community theater, a church choir, or a flower arranging class, Pisces must let that impulse out or lose the spark they're so well known for.

Romance

Romance isn't always about falling in love. Romance may be travel or even a wander through a local forest. It could even be a trip to the second-hand store, knocking off two birds with one stone. Beautiful vintage clothes inspire and light Pisces up and even second-hand clothes nobody else wants, Pisces sees the potential to make something beautiful out of even the lowliest polyester leisure suit. The thrill of the hunt satisfies their curiosity and the thrill of finding what they didn't even imagine they needed to add to their wardrobe or home décor repertoire, even more so.

For Pisces, when romance isn't about love, it's about the open road, or air travel to faraway, exotic places. Living their dreams is a huge motivating force for Pisces, taking them to distant, unknown places, where their only communicative tool is their brilliant smile and warm personality. Experiences and the lessons that come with them are one of the best things in life, where Pisces is concerned. These add to their natural storehouse of riches, further enhancing the mysterious wisdom of this sign.

For Pisces, there's nothing like seeing something few have seen or that they've waited to see their entire lives. My Pisces friend, for example, remembers her father taking her to the Louvre in Paris as a child. She'd always wanted to see the Mona Lisa, and standing before it on that special day is one of her most cherished childhood memories.

But when romance is about love, take care of the heart of Pisces. Intensely passionate lovers and partners, they're also deeply loyal. When these qualities are not returned by their partners, Pisces becomes morose to the point of suicide.

It's difficult for tender Pisces to understand why their partner is so incapable of returning their intensity, so think twice about not being straight with your intentions when approaching Pisces. If you're just in it for a fun night, then you'd best be very clear about that, or you may never forget what Pisces will characterize as your dishonesty. You may even discover that you're widely known as a douchebag or a trollop.

Romantic love is, for Pisces, one of the most transcendent experiences of human life. But as they get older, many Pisceans despair of the utilitarian approach to romance far too many people take. They want all the bells and whistles. They want the hearts, the flowers, the waves crashing to shores, the palm trees swaying, and the band playing a tender melody. If you're not that lover, take a pass on Pisces or regret not having done so.

To Pisces, life is one long, romantic adventure. With the Piscean ability to just roll with whatever life throws at them, they adore the surprises and sudden beauty of each day. They know the world is a rude, sharp-elbowed place. They know others don't necessarily understand their sunny smile and faraway eyes. But they don't care. They have lived through all the other signs of the zodiac. That infuses their spirits with an understanding of life's endless sweetness. While this reality makes many believe that Pisces may be a bit absurd their understanding of the romantic tale of life inspires those around them to understand where the Piscean is coming from. It's a tremendous, glorious gift and one we should all aspire to learn how to emulate.

Time to Recharge

Introspective, sensitive Pisces loves to socialize – just not all the time. If Pisces isn't left to find their center in solitude, they may become not only ill but testy. This a sign perfectly happy to sit at home, talking to their pets or creating their next great piece. Being semi-social, you'll see Pisces out and about when they're darned good and ready to do it.

Like a battery that has run down, the Pisces is never alone with their thoughts and can never rest from the world. They often have to recharge their batteries and recycle their energy. That recycling means rest, quiet, and peace; this sign needs to feel truly whole. While enjoying a happy social life and having many friends, Pisces can't be continually with other people.

Because of their intuitive nature, Pisces needs to withdraw to recharge but also to analyze what they've learned in their social interactions, about themselves and about other people.

Reflection in tranquility is how Pisces people rejuvenate themselves, re-creating their spirits. When with other people, too often the energies they intuit, both negative and positive, can deplete them, leaving them in need of rest.

While most of us take other people at face value, Pisces senses and then "reads" the undercurrents that lurk below the surface. They can spot a narcissist, for example, a mile away. This prompts them to run in the other direction, as energy vampires are Piscean kryptonite. But even people they love can wear them out. This is true of best friends, family, lovers, and even spouses and children.

For Pisces to be at their best, they need to let distance make the heart grow fonder. If this isn't understood by their nearest and dearest – and it often isn't – Pisces may rebel. While a nurturing, compassionate sign par excellence, Pisces can also turn off when they're not getting what they need. They can become cold, intolerant, and exhausted from all the human energies swirling around them.

To the rest of us, those energies may seem relatively innocuous. To a Pisces, they're an existential threat. Even a night out dancing can be difficult for Pisces to recover from. They come home over-stimulated and unable to sleep. While they might not want the night to end, they know the price they'll pay in the morning for the revelry they've indulged in.

Bad energies must also be considered. People with less than noble intentions coming into proximity with a Pisces will feel two holes burning into them from across a crowded room. These are the piercing eyes of a Pisces who has pegged them as bad news. Without a word, Pisces will know that these people are not on the menu for them or for anyone they know. That knowledge is not subject to the amendment because when Pisces has "read" ill intent, mendacity, or general nastiness, they will not be changing their vote for any reason.

They know, and while people will often scoff at Piscean intuition, it's invariably the case that their immediate read of others pans out. While those around them will poo-poo these "instant readings," the conclusion that others will inevitably draw is that Pisces' immediate read of the undesirable in question was correct. Not taking Piscean intuition seriously is a major source of frustration for this sign – yet another reason they sometimes need to jump into the depths of the ocean to sit on a rock, looking out to sea when it all gets to be too much.

Honesty and Integrity

The deep spirituality of Pisces is sensitive to those who lie, manipulate and treat others with anything less than respect. While Pisces can respectfully and even forcefully disagree, they will never disagree to the point of abuse.

But when you fail to model honesty and integrity with the sensitive fish, you will find yourself cut off. This is not done to be cruel or to punish. This is done by Pisces, to protect themselves and those around them.

No one likes to talk about this side of Pisces, but the hurt encountered by people under this zodiac sign when you do the wrong thing translates into instant ostracism. You will not speak to your Pisces again if they can help it. Pisces will avoid you until the end of the world when you bring ugliness into their peaceful, compassionate sphere.

It's not even personal with Pisces. With the fish, it's all about damage control. Intuitively equipped to read the hearts of others with precision, those who may cause trouble are distanced. But Pisces only cuts the cord once there's evidence that they were right in their intuition.

Liars are transparent to Pisces, almost at first glance. That man in the corner giving you the side-eye? He's a Pisces who has detected a misalignment between your words and your actions. You've never seen him before. So what? Pisces knows.

Got a hefty ego? Like to throw your weight around? Don't do it in front of that woman sitting at the bar, watching you in the mirror.

She's going to stay as far away from you as possible, and if you get out of line, she'll make sure to tell the others. No offense. Just clean it up.

Honesty and integrity are imperative to Pisces because they know when you're lying, and they know when you're not true to yourself. A Pisces can spot a phony a mile away. And Pisces doesn't like phonies.

Honesty is a virtue that's taken seriously by Pisces. And integrity? Trusting others is right up there, and in the mind of the fish, these are the same thing. If you can't be true to yourself, you'll never be true to others, and that is fundamentally dishonest. Pisces, having moved through all the other sun signs, understands that one of the greatest goals of human life is integrity and to live as you were created to live. People who can't understand this fundamental need of Pisces – to expect the same honesty and integrity from others that they model – needn't come calling.

Respect and Understanding

One of Pisces's greatest challenges is being misunderstood. Many read Pisces as flighty or disengaged from reality. Neither claim is true.

Pisces is a dreamer. That much is true. But Pisces is also a visionary, seeing into the hearts of humans and of matters great and small. That is no mean feat. While the world around Pisces is reaching for answers, Pisces has already arrived at that goal.

But nobody listens. Pisces proposes a solution that sounds impossible or impractical. It is ignored until someone higher up the food chain clues in, and then Pisces is proven right. This may not happen for some time, but the ability of a Piscean to see beyond is usually, if not always, vindicated.

There is no explanation for this phenomenon, but that's immaterial. Once you've witnessed the prognosticating powers of Pisces, you'll never question them again. This is a predominantly third decan quality. However, all Pisces have access to this highly developed intuition, fully formed at the end of the astrological rainbow.

And that demands respect. Just because you can't find an empirical pathway to explain it does not mean to say it's not true. You have eyes and ears. Let them teach you that when Pisces says something that sounds a little crazy, you had best take notice.

Take my Pisces friend, for example. She not only "knew," in that special Pisces way, that Barack Obama would win the presidency and serve two successful terms, she knew it years before he even announced his intention. She knew that cannabis would eventually flourish as both medicine and recreation. When she confided this to a group of political operatives at a campaign training session, she was laughed at.

Who's Laughing Now?

My point is simple - place a bet on a Pisces prediction and get rich. Most people think they're crazy until they think they're geniuses. Wrong on both counts. Pisces are powerful, intuitive thinkers who process creative thinking into predictive accuracy.

So, it's much more about creativity than it is about soothsaying if you're paying attention. When you finally submit to Pisces and their processes, you'll discover a world of out-of-the-box thinking. That is the true impact of the way this sign thinks and acts. Pisces is so far out that they're right on time.

Elon Musk is not a Pisces, but that's where his Neptune lives. You do that math and tell me I'm wrong!

Respect the Pisces. Understand the Pisces and reap spillover generously splashed on you by this gentle, prescient sign. When you know a Pisces as a friend, lover, family member, or colleague, you know a portal to the weirder reaches of the universe. Through that portal are the things others don't see. We suspect the existence of these things, so we make monster movies and write ghost stories and speculative fiction about worlds we imagine might be out there, somewhere. Pisces sees those worlds with a fishy third eye.

But Pisces, if you respect and understand the beauty of a sign that lives in a type of knowledge that's not in a textbook but in the stars and the cells of their bodies, will show you amazing places.

Ultimately, what the Pisces needs more than anything is the freedom to swim in its eternal figure eight, both pulling and pushing, coming and going, being and not being. This mystically invested sign is the terminus of the zodiac, the Omega to Aries' childlike Alpha. Understanding this complex and amazing sign is key to understanding astrology itself.

Conclusion

Thank you for taking this journey with me into the heart of Pisces, the amazing zodiac sign that spiritually and in terms of karma, has seen and done it all.

I sincerely hope you've enjoyed reading more about the fish and how its natives navigate a world they can too often find unwelcoming. The shyness and reticence of this sign are unparalleled in the zodiac. That's perhaps because, on the journey around the astrological wheel, Pisces have learned lessons most of us haven't yet been exposed to.

This book was intended to be more than a look into the many traits and characteristics Pisceans exhibit. It's intended to offer you a grounding in basic astrology and the complex examination of the planets that results in a fuller understanding of individuals born under this sign. That grounding will serve you well as you move forward, hopefully creating your own chart. Maybe you'll become so adept at reading the movements of the planets; you'll become your circle's astrological expert!

Whether you read this book for pleasure or to improve your astrological knowledge, I hope I've been able to deliver both an informative and entertaining read.

Please enjoy the resources, following these few closing words. Don't forget to check out my other works on the signs of the zodiac, containing information specific to each sign, as well as broad astrological understanding.

Here's another book by Mari Silva that you might like

THE ULTIMATE GUIDE TO AN AMAZING
ZODIAC SIGN IN ASTROLOGY

VIRGO

MARI SILVA

Additional Resources

Are you ready to do your chart? Don't forget to obtain the exact time of your birth by obtaining your long-form birth certificate.

There are many places online to have a chart done, but the most reliable of these is undoubtedly Astro.com. This site is excellent for all levels of astrologers, from amateur to veteran. Here, you'll find everything you need!

References

12 Astrology Zodiac Signs Dates, Meanings and Compatibility. (n.d.). Www.Astrology-Zodiac-Signs.Com. https://www.astrology-zodiac-signs.com/

Astrology - All Sun Moon Combinations. (n.d.). Astrology-Numerology.Com. http://astrology-numerology.com/sun-moon.html

Astrology King. (n.d.). Astrology King. http://astrologyking.com

Astrology Library. (n.d.). Astrolibrary.Org. https://astrolibrary.org/

Introduction to Astrology. (n.d.). Www.Astro.Com. https://www.astro.com/astrologie/in_intro_e.htm

Personality & Relationship Astrology: Compatibility, Attraction and Sign Personality Traits. (n.d.). South Florida Astrologer - Personality & Relationship Astrology. https://www.southfloridaastrologer.com/

Rovelli, P. (n.d.). *The Whole Astrology Workbook.* http://astronargon.us/The%20Whole%20Astrology%20Workbook.pdf